The six titles in this series are:

Mountains and Forests

Polar Regions

Tropical Forests

Grasslands

Deserts

Seas and Inland Waters

Animals and their Environment

Animals of the Seas and Inland Waters

Federica Colombo and Gina Barnabé
Illustrated with drawings by Gabriele Pozzi

Burke Books LONDON * TORONTO * NEW YORK

First published in the English language 1982
Revised reprint 1983
© Burke Publishing Company Limited 1982
Translated and adapted from
Gli animali e l'ambiente: Il Mare e le Acque Interne
© Vallardi Industrie Grafiche S.p.A. 1978

CIP data
Colombo, Federica
    Animals of the seas and inland waters. —
    (Animals and their environment)
    1. Marine fauna. — Juvenile literature
    2. Fresh-water fauna. — Juvenile literature
    I. Title   II. Series
    591.92   QL120

    ISBN 0 222 00856 3

Burke Publishing Company Limited
Pegasus House, 116-120 Golden Lane, London EC1Y OTL, England.
Burke Publishing (Canada) Limited
Toronto, Ontario, Canada.
Burke Publishing Company Inc.
540 Barnum Avenue, Bridgeport, Connecticut 06608, U.S.A.
Printed by Vallardi Industrie Grafiche S.p.A. Milan

Acknowledgements

The photographs are reproduced by permission of:

Gaggero; Marka; Mazza and Arch. Vallardi

Contents

The Seas and Coastal Waters   12

The Sea-Bed   14

Physical Characteristics of Water   16

Mankind and the Sea   18

The Exploitation
 of the Sea's Resources   20

Plankton   22

The Food-Chain   24

Fish   26

The Spray and Inter-Tidal Zone   28

The Sandy Bottom   30

The Rocky Bottom   32

The Open Sea and the Ocean Depths   34

Teleostei or Bony Fish   36

Cartilaginous Fish   38

The Abyssal Depths   40

The Birth of an Atoll   42

Life Among the Coral   44

The Art of Camouflage   46

Animal Associations   48

Dangers of the Sea   50

Marine Reptiles   52

Migration   54

Lakes   56

Flora and Fauna of Lakes   58

Rapids, Rivers and Estuaries   60

The Amazon Basin: An Inland Sea   62

Fish and Invertebrates   64

The Pond: A World in Itself   66

Pondlife   68

Birds and Mammals of the Pond   70

Pond Reptiles and Amphibians   72

Animals of the Seas and Inland Waters   74

Index   84

The Seas and Coastal Waters

Seventy per cent of the Earth's surface is covered by water. This water is classified on the basis of its salinity, that is, the amount of sodium chloride and other mineral salts which it contains. There are three main categories: (a) marine, with about thirty-five parts per thousand of salt. (b) fresh, with a maximum of five parts per thousand. (c) brackish water which has a variable concentration of salt and is found in estuaries where fresh water and sea water merge. There is less salt content further up-river from the estuary and it gets saltier nearer the mouth of the river until fully marine conditions are reached in the open sea.

All water, even so-called "fresh" water, contains some dissolved minerals but it is the salt (sodium chloride) content which is the most significant. Sea water also contains salts of potassium and other elements. Within the three categories — marine, fresh and brackish — there will be variations, caused by currents and other factors.

Salinity is higher in warm seas than in colder ones. In the Red Sea, where there is considerable evaporation, a high level — of about forty-three parts per thousand — is found. In contrast, the Baltic Sea which has a low evaporation factor and high inflow of fresh water from rivers has a low salinity of 7.8 parts per thousand. There are great differences between inland seas. The Dead Sea, a land-locked lake in a hot climate, can lose water only by evaporation and the salinity there reaches 240 grammes per litre.

Oceans, Lakes and Rivers

The seas which cover such a great part of the Earth's surface are divided into five major oceans. At the poles there are: in the North, the Arctic Ocean; in the South, the Antarctic Ocean. Between the polar seas are the Atlantic, Indian and Pacific Oceans. These great marine basins are further subdivided as, for instance, the North and South Atlantic. Lakes are generally filled with fresh or only slightly salty water. The largest lakes of the world are: in Asia, the Caspian Sea (438,000 square kilometres) and the Aral Sea; in North America, Lake Superior (83,000 square kilometres), the second largest lake in the world; and, in Africa, Lake Victoria.

The Dead Sea and the Caspian Sea are situated in deep depressions in the Earth's surface and are below sea-level, the Dead Sea at -394 metres and the Caspian -26 metres.

Some of the rivers of the world cover thousands of kilometres before they reach the coast and the sea. The Mississippi-Missouri is the longest of all (6,970 kilometres). Next come the Blue and White Nile (6,671 kilometres long); the Amazon in South America (6,280 kilometres) and the Ob-Irtysh in Russia (5,300 kilometres).

0-200 metres

200-3000 metres

over 3000 metres

Freshwater lakes

Inland seas

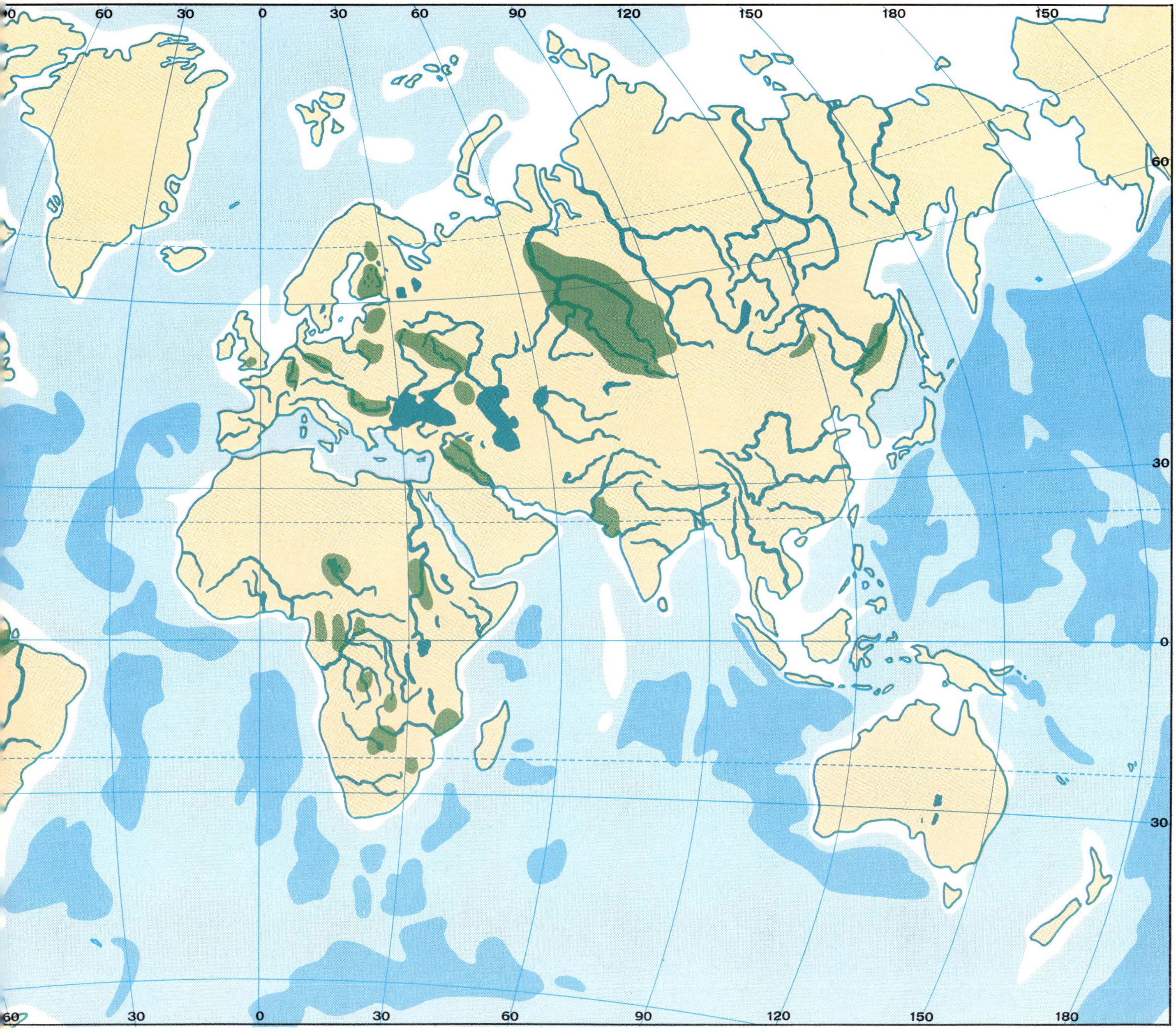
60
30
0
30
60
90
120
150
180
150
60
30
0
30
60
30
0
30
60
90
120
150
180

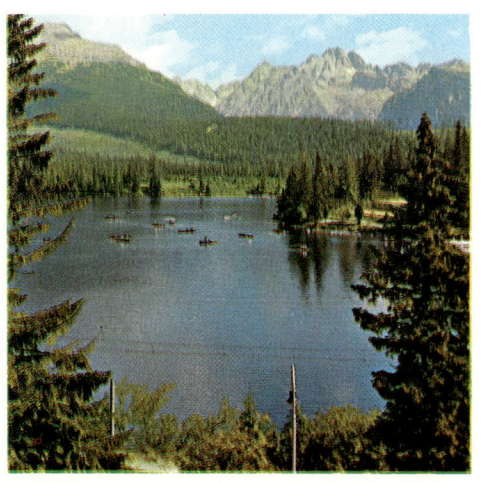

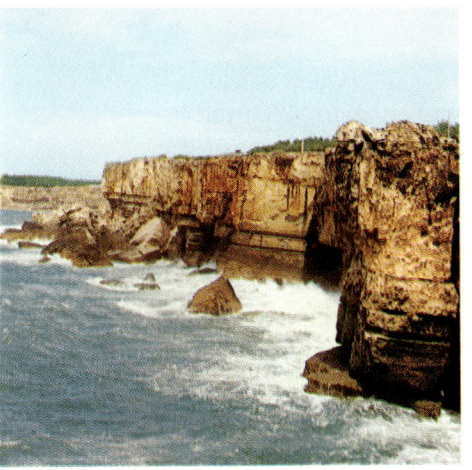

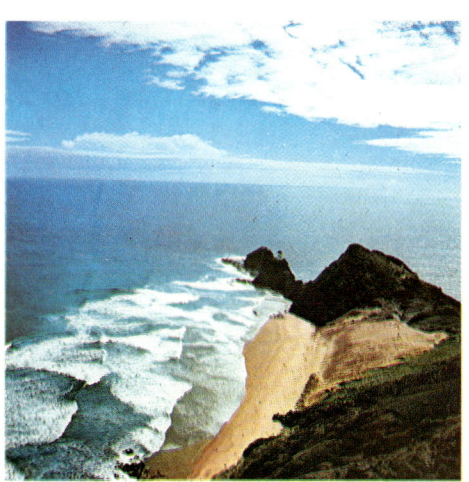

The Sea-Bed

Although looking rather uniform, the sea has a great variety of habitats. These habitats merge into one another with few distinct boundaries. A section of the shore and coastal sea out to the deeper oceans shows a series of major habitats. The shallower water above the continental shelf near to the coast gets gradually deeper until we reach the deep oceans. There are several classifications of the marine environment; one commonly used is the depth of light penetration. The euphotic zone stretches down to a depth of two hundred metres and below this is the aphotic zone, where the light does not penetrate. In the transition from marine to terrestrial environment there are two divisions: the littoral (or tidal) zone where the animals and plants are subjected to periods of submergence and exposure each day; and above this, the coastal area above the high-tide line which is usually dry but is reached by spray during gales.

Structure of the Sea-Bed

Our knowledge of the sea-bed is largely derived from indirect observations based on geophysical measurements (gravity, seismic and acoustic). Only a few details have been learned by direct observation from underwater vessels.

The continental shelf has been

SHALLOW SEA (Neritic Zone)   OPEN SEA (Pelagic Zone)

LITTORAL FAUNA   PELAGIC FAUNA

Rocks

Euphotic Zone

SANDY BENTHOS

200 m

CONTINENTAL SHELF

CONTINENTAL SLOPE

Aphotic Zone

PROFUNDAL FAUNA

PROFUNDAL BENTHOS

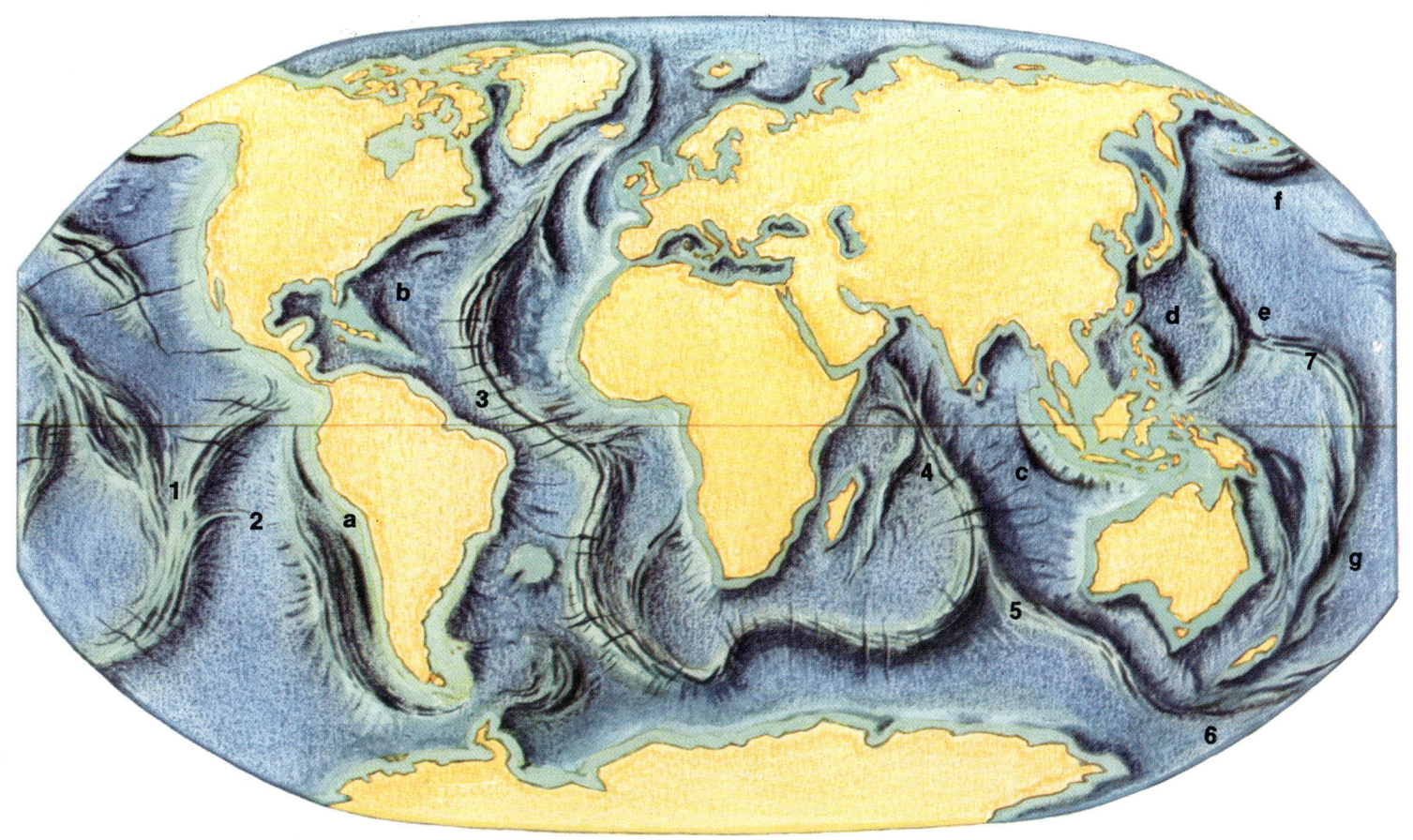

Facing page: *The diagram shows a cross-section of the coast and illustrates how the continental shelf slopes down gradually to two hundred metres. Next comes the continental escarpment and finally the ocean-bed. Also shown are the euphotic zone, illuminated by the sun's rays, and the aphotic zone which is dark and inhabited only by predators.*

Oceanic Ridges

1. Mid-Pacific
2. East Pacific
3. Mid-Atlantic
4. Mid-Indian
5. Indian Antarctic
6. Pacific Antarctic
7. Hawaiian

Oceanic Trenches

a. Peru-Chile
b. Puerto Rican
c. Andaman
d. Philippines
e. Marianas
f. Aleutian
g. Kermadec

mapped by means of seismic instruments and other techniques. The sea-bed is in fact an extension of the ground's surface beneath sea-level down to a depth of two hundred metres. The continental shelf extends on average to seventy kilometres from the coastline. It includes under-sea valleys, basins and rocky peaks — which form islands where they penetrate the surface. Towards the open sea the steepness of the shelf's gradient increases dramatically until the continental escarpment is reached and this plunges to a depth of two thousand metres very quickly.

In the ocean depths there are mountains and ridges just like those in the land surfaces. In the central Atlantic the great mid-Atlantic ridge which winds from Labrador in the north to the Antarctic in the south is roughly S-shaped and divides the Atlantic into two more or less parallel basins. Many regularly formed ridges divide the Pacific into four main basins and provide the base of atolls. There are deep trenches in the ocean beds (between 6,000 metres and 11,000 metres deep). These are always situated along the borders of sunken lands, never in the middle of the oceans.

The deepest trenches are in the Pacific: the Marianas (-11,022 metres), the Philippines (-10,497 metres), and the Tongan (-10,882 metres). The deepest Atlantic trench is the Puerto Rican (-9,220 metres).

Physical Characteristics of Water

Water is a very special liquid mineral of immense importance for life on Earth. It occurs naturally in three different forms, each of which can be changed into the other through its first form, liquid. The other two are the solid form (ice) and the gaseous form (water vapour). In the liquid form it is more dense than air and the further underwater you go, the greater the pressure. Pressure increases tremendously with depth. Animals which normally live in deep water under great pressure literally burst if brought to the surface.

The density of water changes with temperature and it is at its most dense (heaviest) at about 4°Centigrade at normal atmospheric pressure. Above or below this temperature its density diminishes. This means that water at 0°Centigrade, which is the least dense, rises to the surface where it forms the solid or ice stage. With only the surface frozen, life can go on beneath the ice. Even during the coldest weather the bottom of a pond will not freeze. Water is important to all living creatures but, because it is more dense than air, water can support some of the weight of the animals that live in it. This means that they can often be larger than is possible on land, or they can have a much lighter supporting structure or skeleton. The jellyfish is obviously an animal which, while able to live in water, collapses out of water and soon dies.

Water in mass, such as lakes or the seas, is important as a heat-store because it has a high thermal capacity.

The heat in the sun's rays which penetrate into the water gradually raise its temperature. Lakes and the seas therefore act as a vast store of energy (heat) which they can release gradually into the atmosphere and this has a considerable influence on climate.

The sun's rays consist of light of different wavelengths in the spectrum. If passed through a prism they can be broken up into all the colours of the rainbow. The important but invisible rays are found at the two opposite ends of the rainbow (red and violet). These include the short-wave ultra-violet and the long-wave infra-red rays. The latter are at the "heat" end of the spectrum. The ultra-violet rays are the ones which turn our skin brown in the sunshine and cause sunburn. Ultra-violet in excess is very dangerous and will destroy unicellular creatures. The sunlight falling on the water is broken up into its different colours by the water and the visible and invisible rays have different penetrating powers.

The Origin of Life in Water

One currently popular theory is that when life on Earth began, more than three thousand million years ago, the planet's atmosphere contained nitrogen, ammonia, carbon dioxide, water vapour and many other gases, but no oxygen. The ozone layer (which now envelops the Earth and filters off much of the dangerous ultra-violet radiation) was not present, since there was no oxygen in the atmosphere. Thus, as long as large quantities

of the harmful ultra-violet rays reached the surface, life on land was not possible. However, in the water, the ultra-violet is absorbed very rapidly and does not penetrate far. Therefore, life could develop in this watery medium and the first living organism appeared. Gradually, with the production of oxygen, the increase of this and the related gas ozone in the atmosphere began to provide a protective layer, cutting off some of the

This diagram shows the theoretical capacity of the various rays which make up the sun's (white) light, to penetrate perfectly pure water. The maximum depth (about 240 metres) is reached by violet light; this is also the deepest level at which plants are capable of photosynthesis using chlorophyll. The penetration of visible light through the water increases as you pass from red through yellow to the blue wavelengths, but the wavelengths corresponding to infra-red and ultra-violet are almost all absorbed near the surface.

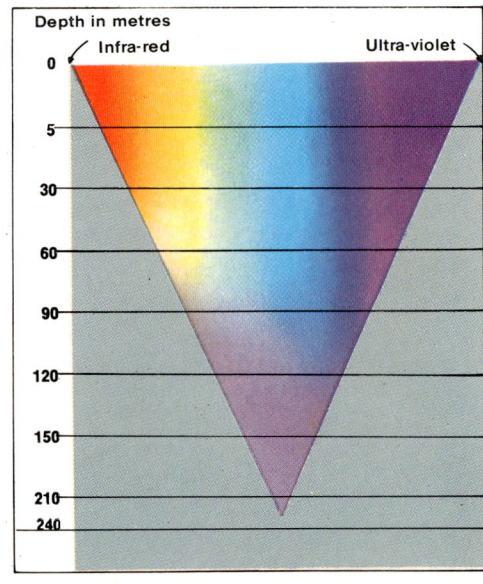

LIGHT PENETRATION

harmful ultra-violet rays. As the ultra-violet rays decreased, so life became possible on land.

Wave Movement and Currents

As well as tides, which are the periodic rising and falling of sea-levels caused by the action of the moon's gravitational pull, other character-istic movements of water-masses are currents and waves, both of which occur in seas and lakes.

Currents are the movement of one part of a water mass in relation to the remainder. Such movements, which in the seas can cover immense areas over thousands of kilometres, are caused by wind or by differences in temperature or salinity between water masses at different depths.

Wind action has the greatest effect on lakes, whereas temperature and sal-inity differences move enormous masses of sea-water for thousands of

kilometres (for example, the Labrador current and the Gulf Stream).

Wave movement, on the other hand, is a rhythmic rising and falling and not just a horizontal shifting of the upper strata of water. Therefore, tides which affect the total water-mass, must be distinguished from currents which are vertical or horizontal movements of parts of the water.

While wave action on the beach helps to oxygenate the water and to dissolve out minerals in the sand and rocks, the tremendous pounding and tearing action provides problems for the animals and plants living there.

Wind direction

This diagram illustrates wave movement. The gull demonstrates the result of the rotary movement of a water molecule and is, in fact, only moving up and down. The wave motion moves but the actual water-mass in the deep sea moves only slightly.

Wave movement

Mankind and the Sea

The sky, space, planets and the stars have always fascinated Man. Although it is only recently that men have been able to travel in space, the stars have been seriously studied for hundreds of years. It is strange that the exploration of the ocean's depths is still in the same pioneer stage as space travel. Now the sea-bed is being studied in all its aspects. Two things have stimulated this exploration. The discovery of minerals, such as natural gas and oil, with their economic value and importance to the modern economy; and the ever-increasing demand for protein-rich food for the growing population of the world.

Deep Sea Exploration

Modern technology has developed advanced vessels for undersea exploration. They range from oceanographic ships to underwater diving-bells, from bathyscopes to underwater houses.

Modern oceanographic ships are floating laboratories where scientists can make direct observations. Research can be carried out on the structure of the ocean-bed, using echo-sounders; and probes can be used for gathering geological samples. The direction and influences of marine currents can be studied, so that we can better understand the changes of climate.

Underwater observations can be carried out by frogmen to depths of eighty metres. With diving equipment the range increases to three hundred metres. To descend to the depths, some submarine vessel is needed to protect the divers from the

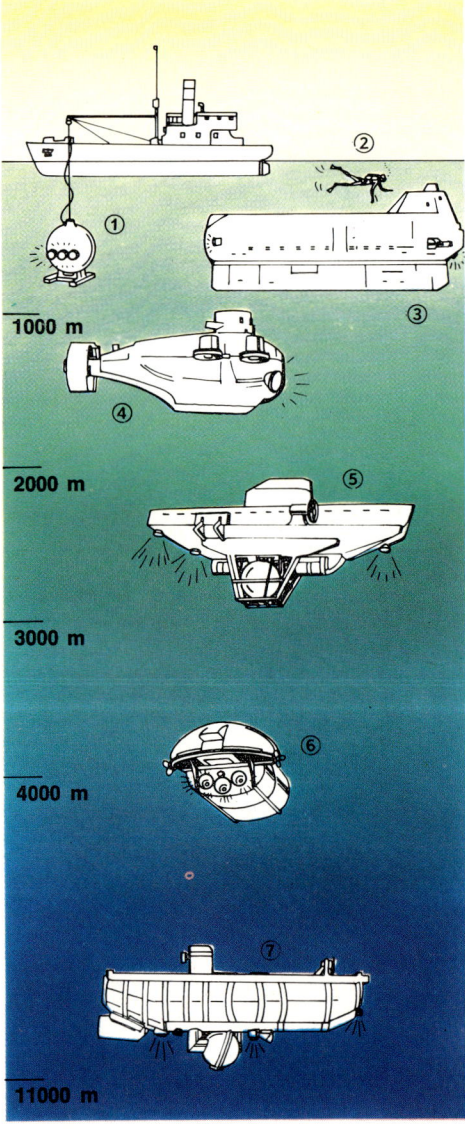

pressure. In these craft a team can take down cameras, and probes for bringing samples of soil and rock to the surface.

Underwater exploration

1. The bathysphere, Beebe-Barton (932 metres)
2. Frogmen
3. Research submarine, Ben Franklin (up to 1,000 metres)
4. Bathymobile Alvin (1,200 metres)
5. Bathyscope FNRS 111 (2,300 metres)
6. Bathymobile Deepstar (up to 4,000 metres)
7. Bathyscope Trieste (10,911 metres)

Underwater exploration equipment can be divided into three groups according to the depths they reach. In the first group, which can descend to a depth of five hundred metres, belongs Star, fitted with manoeuvrable external arms used for manipulation. Depths of fifteen hundred metres have been reached by two-man submarines Alvin and Deep Quest. Deeper waters are reached by much more sophisticated equipment such as the Trieste, which can descend to more than ten thousand metres, carrying a three-man team. It is fitted with three television cameras and has external arms for collecting samples. It can remain submerged for up to ten hours.

Underwater houses invented by the Frenchman Jacques Cousteau and tested to a depth of between twelve and fifty metres are used to study Man's reaction to living for long periods underwater and also to conduct serious experiments on the possibilities of exploiting the sea-bed. The American Sea-labs can remain submerged for fifteen hundred hours at a depth of 180 metres and are filled with a mixture of nitrogen, helium and oxygen. Right: A typical example of a submarine laboratory, built three hundred metres below the surface, off the Virgin Islands.

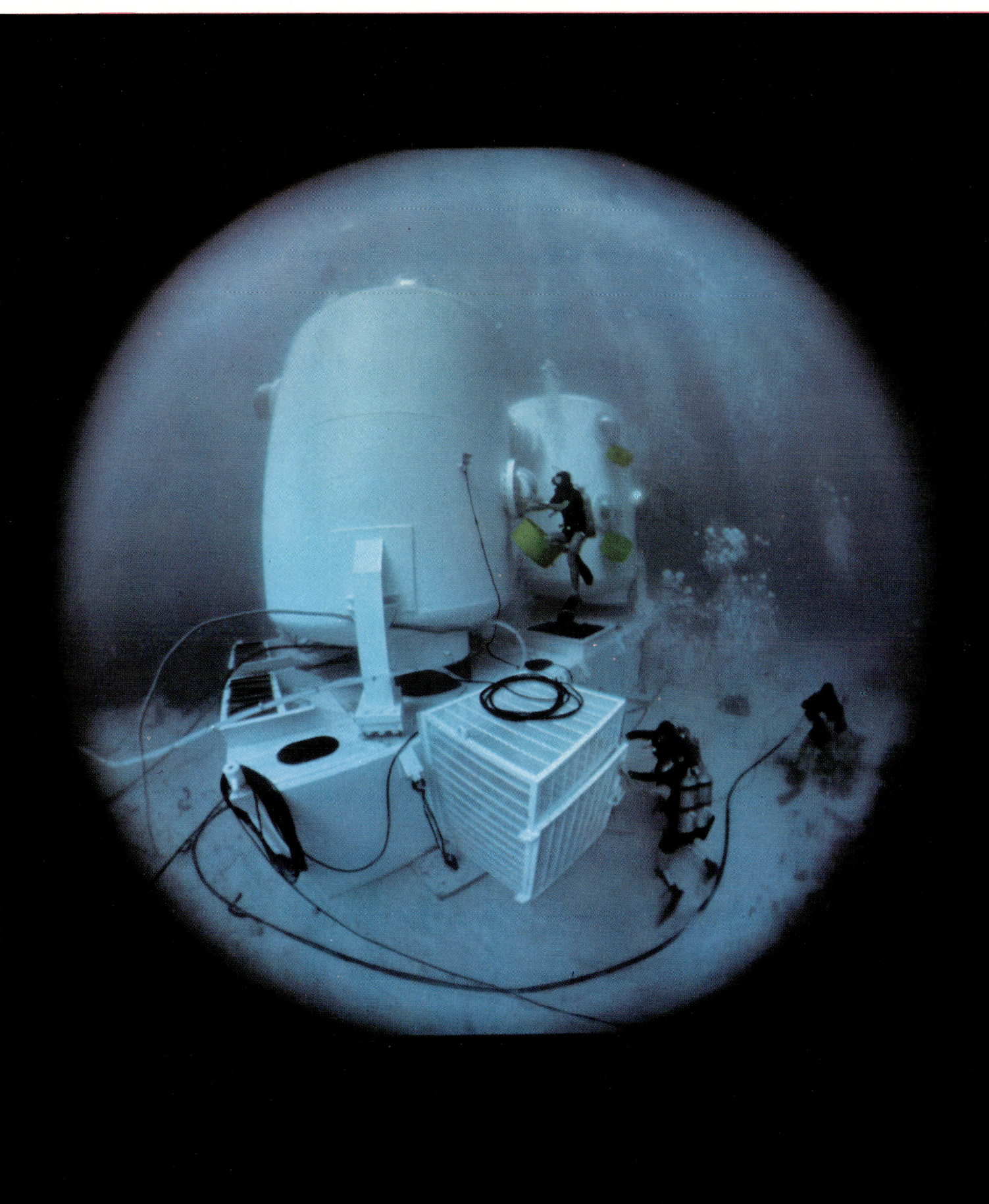

The Exploitation of the Sea's Resources

The traditional method of tunny-fishing in the Mediterranean. Hooks and nets are used successfully for large catches. These methods are dying out elsewhere in Europe as modern boats and equipment are introduced to satisfy the greater demands of the canning and freezing industries.

The Sea, a Diminishing Larder

The sea has always provided food for mankind and its resources were confidently believed to be inexhaustible. However, sometimes the benefits of modern economy have brought disaster in their train. The seas have become the sewers of the industrial nations, with sewage and chemical waste from factories spilling into the rivers and then into the sea, killing many of the organisms on which the fish feed.

Oil is discharged into the sea, polluting it and causing destruction of animal life.

At the same time fishing has become industrialized. Factory freezer-ships which act as parent ships to fleets of fishing-boats are equipped with sophisticated instruments to locate the shoals of fish. As the factory-ships can clean, freeze and pack the catch, the fishermen can stay out of port for much longer and can go to fishing-grounds that are much further away and take far more fish than is needed, and far more than the fish population can stand. Many fish are taken which will become animal food or fertilizer. Some species are becoming rare. Mackerel and sardines have completely disappeared from some fishing-grounds where they used to be abundant. The threat to the world's sea-food supplies has finally been realized and many nations are working on schemes to conserve fishing-grounds and increase the supply of fish. Agreements about fishing-rights and quotas may be difficult to arrange but, in the meantime, aquaculture is growing in importance. This involves the breeding of marine creatures as intensively as cattle or poultry on land. A sea area is chosen and treated with fertilizers to encourage the growth of the phytoplankton on which so many marine animals feed. The Japanese have also been successfully breeding crayfish for many years. The eggs of this crustacean are laid in tanks. The larvae are fed initially on phytoplankton. Later, they feed on minute crustaceans and then on fish pieces. When the crayfish have reached maturity they are sold either on the open market or to the canning industry. Shellfish farming is particularly important as the shellfish filter and absorb polluted water as they feed. Aquaculture means that they can grow in carefully maintained tanks of unpolluted water. Mussels are grown particularly successfully in Spain. Salmon are raised in this way until they grow to a migratory age and then they are released into the sea.

Swordfish are fairly common in the Atlantic and the Mediterranean. In the Straits of Messina, where the fishing is intensive, lookouts perched at the top of the masts of the fishing-boats direct the fishermen towards the swordfish.

Plankton

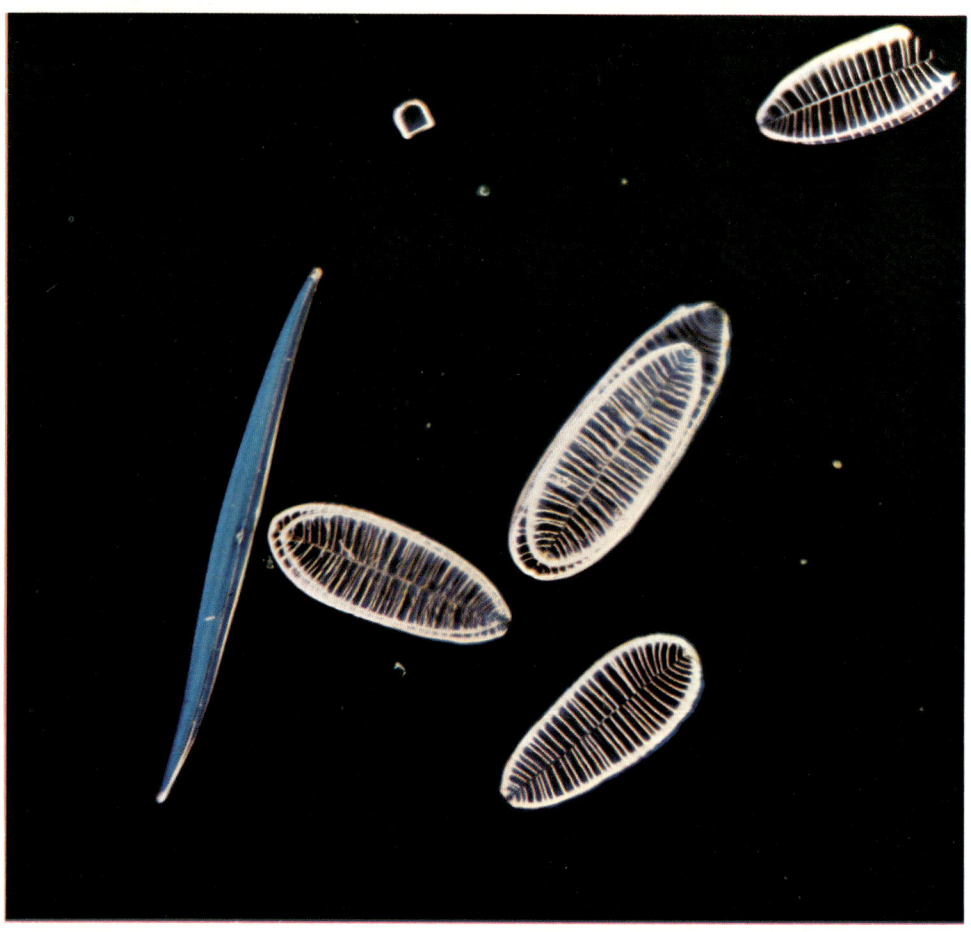

Diatoms are the most abundant plants of all marine plankton. Protected by a hard siliceous shell they are kept afloat by the presence of very small quantities of oil. They reproduce by splitting into two cells, each of which retains a part of the original shell and uses this as a basis for completing its own protective covering.

What is Plankton?

Marine plankton consists of microscopic organisms, both plant and animal. Being very buoyant, they rise up to the surface in the day and sink during the night. They are carried along by the sea's currents and, although they are found in all seas, the numbers vary. They are most abundant near coasts and in colder and temperate seas. To increase their numbers they need certain minerals but these are not evenly distributed throughout the oceans. Plankton is vitally important as the organisms form the first link in the marine food-chain. Phytoplankton consists of plants. Zooplankton consists of animals, and may include either adults or young stages.

Phytoplankton

Like its terrestrial counterparts, marine vegetation is essential for the development of life in the seas. Through photosynthesis the microscopic plants convert inorganic matter into complex organic substances. Water, carbon dioxide and various mineral salts are transformed into sugars. These are then converted into starches, fats and proteins by the plant's various processes. In photosynthesis plants produce more oxygen than they need; they release the surplus into their surroundings. This makes an important contribution both to the sea and to the atmosphere. Over the vast oceans, oxygen is constantly being produced by the phytoplankton.

Microscopic Algae

Diatoms are the most abundant type of marine plankton. They are so small that one litre of sea water can contain hundreds of thousands of them. In the Spring they are so numerous that they colour the sea a dark greeny-brown. Next in importance are the dinoflagellates — single-cell organisms which have both plant and animal characteristics. Some species contain chlorophyll and produce sugars by photosynthesis; others trap very small prey. Both types move with the aid of minute thread-like flagellae which propel them along. Many species are luminous and, when present in large numbers, turn the sea phosphorescent at night. One of the common species is *Noctiluca* which causes tiny flashes of light at sea and can be seen even on the shore on wet sand. As with terrestrial vegetation, phytoplankton varies in composition depending on location and season.

Zooplankton

Zooplankton consists of a large variety of species. They are divided into two groups: the "permanent" zooplankton, those animals which spend their entire lives as marine plankton, such as the Copepods (Crustacea) and the Salps (Urochordata); and the "temporary" ones which spend part of their life-cycle as plankton, such as Sea Urchins, crustacean larvae and fish eggs, etc. Zooplankton also has a varied distribution and is subject to seasonal fluctuations caused largely by variations in temperature.

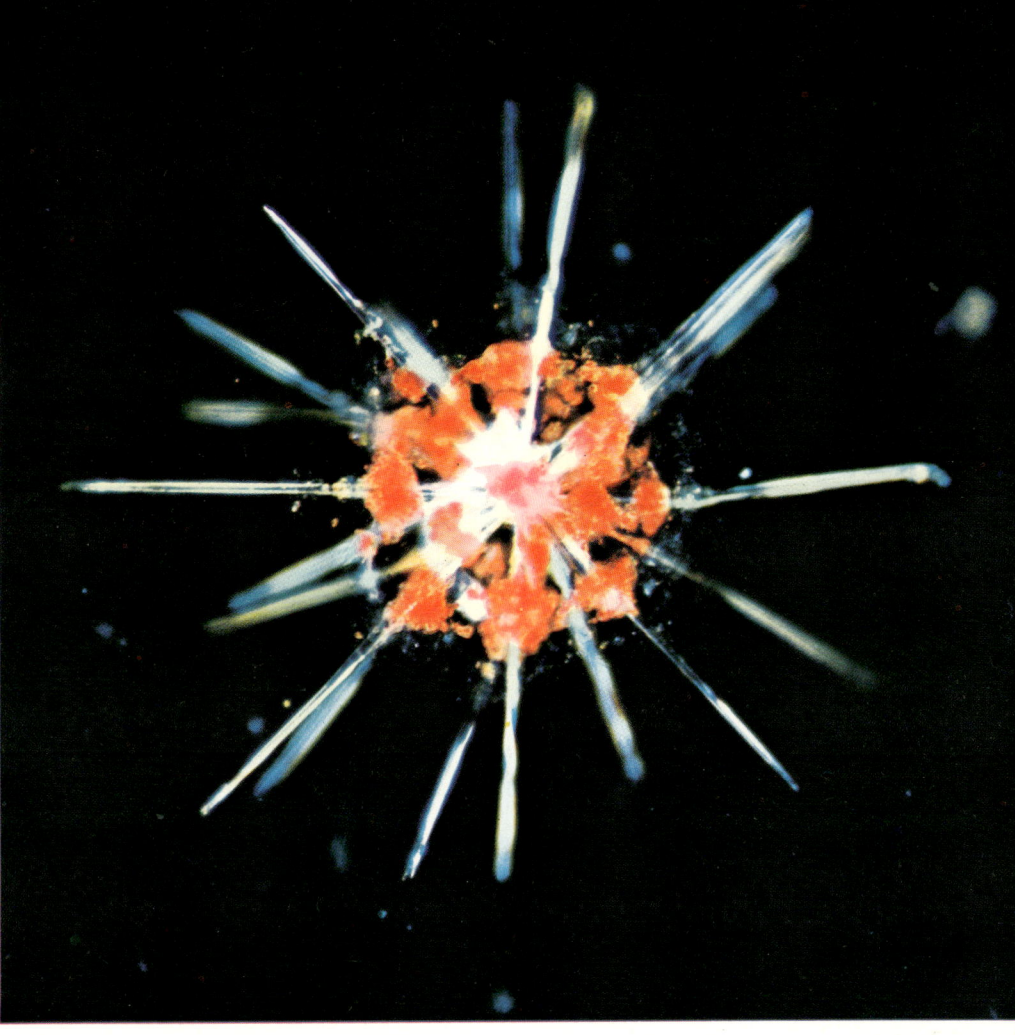

Radiolarians, such as the Ancanthometron *(above), are marine planktonic protozoa. They have a skeleton of silica or of strontium sulphate which, on the death of the organism, falls to the sea-bed and forms radiolarial mud. The whole animal is radially symmetrical.*

Below right: *The larva of a decapod crustacean. Some creatures are only temporary members of the plankton – during the larva phase or the initial stages of their growth. This applies to many fish, crustaceans and molluscs.*

Right: *Copepods are present in vast numbers in marine zooplankton. They are very small crustaceans, a maximum of two millimetres in length. The two large projections on the head aid movement whilst the others are used for respiration and for trapping food.*

The Food-Chain

Frigate Bird

Gannet

Edible Mussel

Lobster

In the sea, as on land, animals depend ultimately on plants which are the primary producers of food in an elaborate food-chain. On land, the plants are mostly large and obvious, such as grasses and bushes, although algae and other smaller plants are present but less obvious.

In the sea, although the seaweeds are obvious, it is the minute unicellular green algae, invisible to the naked eye, which are important. These are present in countless millions and probably produce more oxygen between them than is produced by all the land-plants. Just like the land-plants, these tiny marine algae are green with chlorophyll and with this they synthesize sugars through a similar photosynthetic process. This process combines carbon dioxide and water with the energy provided by sunlight and the plants' chlorophyll to produce (from these simple inorganic substances) more complex organic molecules. The algae are therefore the primary producers and they provide food for the myriads of tiny animals — the zooplankton. As well as the unicellular algae, there are many filamentous ones performing similar processes; the larger of these are seaweeds. Seaweeds may grow many metres long but even so these giant algae are more closely related to microscopic plankton than to flowering plants. The algae in the sea, like the plants on land, are eaten by herbivores, which may be, for example, crabs or other fish. These form the food for dolphins, sharks and marine birds. A few of the large animals in the sea are an exception to the food-chain. The giant Whalebone Whales feed directly on the plankton, sieving out vast quantities as they swim through it.

The plant-life in the sea is obviously limited by the presence of light and the animals that depend on it are similarly restricted. In the black abyssal depths, without light, only predators such as Angler Fish, scavengers and "decomposers" (the organisms which feed on the remains of other animals) can live.

Seagulls

Albatross

Devil Fish

Flying-Fish

Swordfish

Dolphins

Whale

Shark

Tunny

Gilthead

Barnacles

Squid

Sea Bream

Turtle

Crab

Sea Urchin

Sea Anemone

Fish

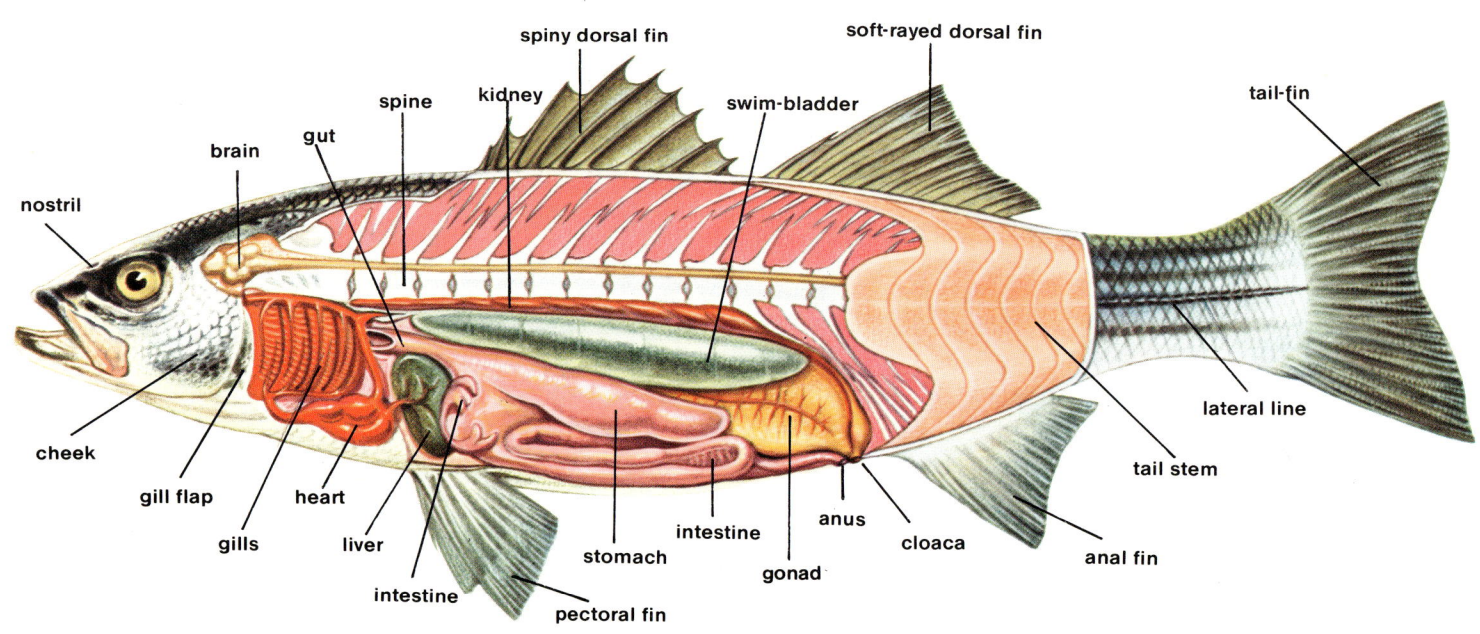

spiny dorsal fin
soft-rayed dorsal fin
spine
kidney
swim-bladder
tail-fin
brain
gut
nostril
cheek
gill flap
heart
gills
liver
intestine
pectoral fin
stomach
intestine
gonad
anus
cloaca
anal fin
tail stem
lateral line

Their Structure and Function

Fish are cold-blooded vertebrates which live in water, breathe through gills and propel themselves by means of the muscular action of the body and fins. Most have a "streamlined" shape for effortless swimming; others have adapted to particular conditions by having very modified shapes. In this way slender fish, such as eels, have evolved. By living close to the sea-bed, they can conceal themselves more easily amongst the seaweed because of their shape. There are also flatfish, such as soles, which live on the sea-bed. Their eyes are both on the same side of the body and they lie on their blind side in the mud of the sea-bed.

Fish move by undulating their bodies and tails, rather like snakes, thrusting against the water's resistance. As they move, the dorsal and anal fins act as stabilizing organs, while the ventral and pectoral fins act as rudders and brakes. Bony fish have a swim-bladder which assists their buoyancy. This is a special sac containing gas. It can expand and contract and, as it effectively changes the specific weight of the fish, it allows the fish to rise to the surface when it is full and to sink when it is empty.

In some cartilaginous fish, such as the shark, the absence of a swim-bladder means that they must always keep swimming, otherwise they would sink to the depths and be killed by the pressure.

The "Voice" of the Fish

Suprisingly enough, the underwater world is not silent. Aquaria, both freshwater and sea-water, give such an impression of silence that we do not expect sounds from fish but, in fact, they do produce quite a wide range of sounds. One of the most common is caused by friction between two parts of the fish's body, such as the spines of the fins.

The fish popularly known as Grunt Fish emit a kind of low grumble. This is produced by a gas-bladder which acts as a resonance chamber. The sunfish, like many other species, grinds its teeth. These noises have various significances: some are a means of communication; others are a warning to predators. They are also used as an echo system to enable the fish to locate their food and other floating objects.

eel

sole

boxfish

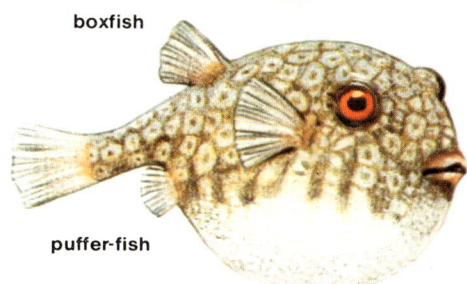

puffer-fish

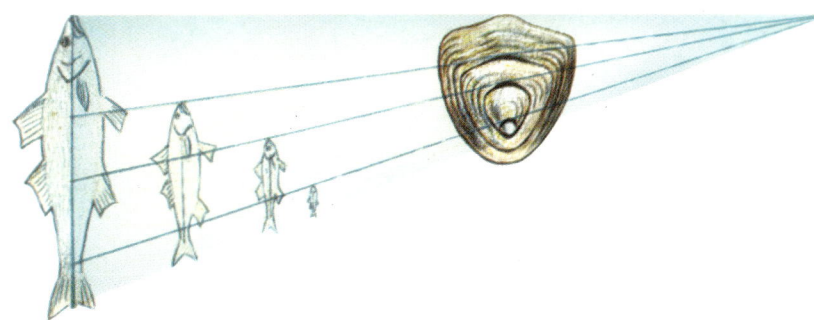

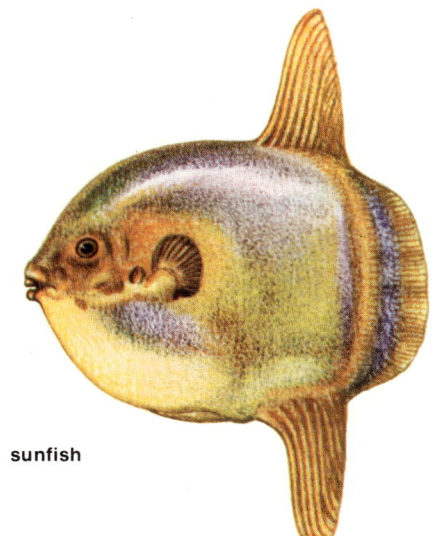

sunfish

Above: The scales which completely cover a fish's body are plate-like lamellae which differ in shape and size according to species. In cartilaginous fish, such as sharks, these consist of cutaneous denticles (placoid scales). Some very rare species have flat rhomboid-shaped scales covered in a luminous substance. Cycloid scales are smooth and circular while the ctenoid scales are also circular but have a spiny posterior margin. Some fish, such as eels, have such small scales that they seem to be missing. Lampreys lack scales altogether. The skins of some fish have poisonous glands. In addition, most fish have a protective mucus cover which is produced from special glands. Scales are never changed but grow during the summer forming concentric circles. They can sometimes be a guide to assessing the age of a fish and this is particularly useful with salmon.

The passage of water over the gills.

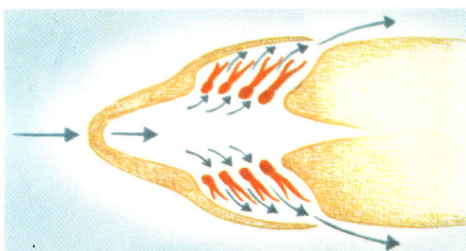

Gills are made of lamellae full of blood capillaries attached to a semi-circular bone. In bony fish, they are protected externally by the operculum; it is absent in cartilaginous fish. The gills are continuously covered with water inhaled by the fish through its mouth. The oxygen extracted from the water by the gills passes into the blood capillaries and then to all parts of the body. At the same time, carbon dioxide is exhaled with the water through the gill openings.

Enlarged diagram of the structure of the lateral line (longitudinal section).
1) sensitive cells; 2) channel full of mucus; 3) nerve; 4) scales.

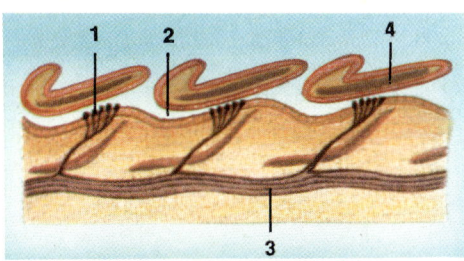

Fish are provided with a kind of sixth sense by the lateral line – a line which is visible on the sides of many fish. This line, which joins the operculum to the tail-fin contains rows of sense organs sensitive to water vibration. It is used to detect the presence of other living organisms. It consists of a longitudinal channel full of mucus, connected to the exterior of the fish by surface tubes which pass through the scales and by the sensitive cells on the walls of the channel which converge on a single nerve connected to the brain.

As well as the typical streamlined shape, fish come in all shapes and sizes. They adapt and evolve according to their environment and their behaviour. Above: Examples of five different shapes: snake-like – eels; flat – sole; boxfish; puffer-fish; and discoids – sunfish.

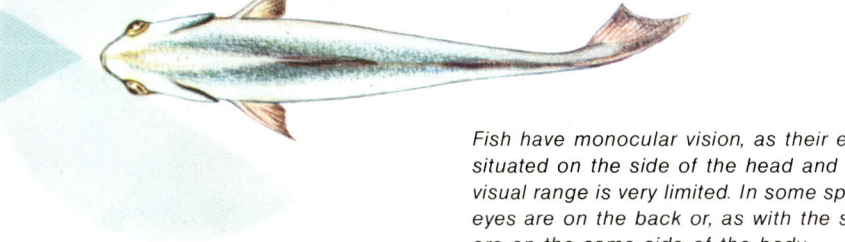

Fish have monocular vision, as their eyes are situated on the side of the head and their visual range is very limited. In some species the eyes are on the back or, as with the sole, both are on the same side of the body.

The Spray and Inter-Tidal Zone

Left: *Barnacles are perhaps the most typical of the tide-line animals. They are crustaceans which attach themselves to rocks and even to the shells of molluscs. To survive during low tides they close their calcareous shells, retaining inside enough moisture to keep them alive until the next high tide.*

The land side of this transitional zone between the land and the sea is splashed regularly by spray and is inhabited by species of both land-living and marine animals. Next comes an area which is covered by the tide twice a day, inhabited by crustaceans (such as crabs and barnacles) and molluscs (such as mussels and limpets) and where there are many types of lichen and algae encrusted on the rocks.

Even here, the plant and animal life can be divided again. Those living on the part of the shore that is only covered at high tide are better adapted for life out of water and include insects which shelter under rocks when the tide comes in. At the low-tide level are those creatures which can only survive out of water for very short periods, such as Sea-Urchins. Sandy shores seem safe habitats for small marine creatures but strong

Far left: *Limpets are a type of mollusc which attach themselves to the rocks in the inter-tidal zone. To do this they secrete a glutinous liquid which is so effective that a force equal to ten kilograms is needed to remove them.*

Left: *Two typical shore creatures; an active crab and an immobile limpet.*

wave movements continually shift the sands and make it an impossible area for all the forms of life which attach themselves to rocks and stones. It is an environment which favours animals which can move easily with the waves and currents and those which can resist the waves. They generally succeed in doing this by burrowing into the sand. Among the animals which make their homes in the sand are burrowing crustaceans and worms, particularly the polychaetes or bristleworms. The intertidal zone is rich in seaweeds which anchor themselves to the rocks to resist the wave action. They provide a habitat for many inter-tidal animals and their thick strands help to retain the moisture under the tangled masses during low tide. The presence of a good cover of seaweed is associated with rocky shores where the weed can anchor itself, whereas sandy or muddy shores are unsuitable for them. In the more sheltered rock pools other species of seaweeds grow.

Above: *Kittiwakes are entirely dependent on the sea for their survival. Although they are excellent fliers and swimmers, they do not dive for their food. They feed on small fish, crustaceans and small animals in the plankton. On shore, they will eat insects. They are essentially cliff-nesting gulls and only come ashore in the breeding-season or when driven by a storm. They are the most maritime of the commoner gulls and are rarely found inland.*

Below: *The cormorant probably derives its name from an ancient French adaptation of the Latin* Corvus marinus, *"Sea Crow". It has black plumage with a purplish sheen. Different species of cormorant are found throughout the world. They feed exclusively on fish which they pursue underwater. They fly rapidly, usually low over the water, and can often be seen sitting on rocks with their wings spread.*

The Sandy Bottom

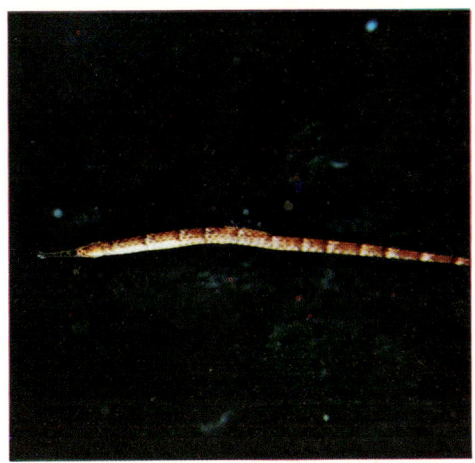

The starfish has a flat, flexible body with five or more arms covered in spines and tubercles. Its mouth is situated on the underside at the centre of the body disc. It moves slowly along the sea-bed using the rows of tube-feet under the arms. Astropecten (left) travels between thirty and sixty centimetres every minute. It does not like light. Astropecten is a carnivorous creature and has specially adapted chemical "receivers" by means of which it detects its prey even at a considerable distance. It eats living or dead organisms which it grasps with its tentacles. Once it has caught its prey the starfish manoeuvres its stomach onto its victim. This stomach is full of digestive juices which the starfish releases to dissolve tissue; food is only swallowed after the digestive process is complete. In the photograph, the starfish is upside down and is in the process of righting itself.

Below: The Peacock Worm is a species of annelid worm which lives in the sandy bottom of the shore and in sandy sea. It usually lives on sandy beds in a rigid tube which it constructs. Its diet is the minute micro-organisms which it first filters from the seawater by means of the brightly-coloured threads of its tentacled crown and then places in its mouth using small hair-like tentacles. When covered with seawater it expands its tentacles (as in the photograph) and the movement of seawater across the tentacles brings the food.

Above: Both the pipefish (left) and the seahorse belong to the order Solenichthyes. Even when dried up, these unusual species retain their shapes because of a structure of tiny bones in their bodies. These fish have no ventral fins but they have long tubular snouts containing a small toothless mouth. Unlike other fish, the seahorse swims in a vertical position and can curl its longish prehensile tail around algae and coral. On the stomach of the male seahorse is a pocket, the brood pouch, in which the female places her fertilized eggs and where they are incubated.

Below: The Common Cuttlefish, Sepia, normally lives in sandy areas, usually in fairly shallow waters. They are mainly active by night. They are predators and have tentacles for catching fish, mussels and crayfish. In turn, they are hunted by marine mammals. The cuttlefish normally moves slowly by means of lateral fins; but, when necessary, it can travel at a much greater speed by using its "funnel" or "syphon" organ. Using this organ the cuttlefish, contracts, compressing the water in its body and expelling it with considerable force, with the result that it moves backwards with force. The cuttlefish hides from predators by emitting a cloud of dark ink-like substance.

Above: The plaice is a species of benthic fish – one which never leaves the sea-bed. When fully grown its body is very flat and asymmetrical; one side is multicoloured and contains both eyes, the other is almost colourless. Unlike the adults, the young fish have a normal bilateral symmetry, with one eye on each side; they are planktonic and swim in the same way as all other fish. In the course of their transformation into adult fish, the young fish undergo certain changes: one eye moves towards the other and colour pigment forms on the same side.

Below: The Common Necklace Shell, Natica alderi, is a mollusc with a smooth dark red spotted exterior. Its body is more or less oval in shape; slim tentacles protrude from its head. They are tactile organs which also carry the eyes. The radula, a rasp-like organ, scrapes off the algae on which the animal lives.

The Rocky Bottom

Left: *Sea-urchins are entirely benthic animals, living on the rocks in deeper water. They are very common on the coasts of Mediterranean countries. They sometimes completely cover whole rocks but many species live in rock crevices. The action of their spines and teeth can sometimes widen the cracks in the rocks. A typical excavator (above left) is the* Paracentrotus lividus *which excavates its own permanent living-quarters. Occasionally this Sea Urchin outgrows its hole and becomes wedged inside. It is then dependent on food being carried into the hole by seawater. Sea Urchins move along the ocean bottom on tube-feet. They are generally omnivorous and, notwithstanding their spikes and poisonous filaments, are often eaten by other animals such as large crustaceans and starfish.*

On the rocky sea-bed there are many different species of crustaceans. One of the commonest is the Spiny Lobster (left). It is particularly common along the Atlantic coast from Senegal to the British Isles and is also found in lesser numbers in the Mediterranean. It lives at depths of up to one hundred metres and feeds on Sea Urchins and bivalve molluscs. In the larval stage they form part of the plankton; after several metamorphic changes, they assume their final form and from then on are benthic. Adult crustaceans have a rigid exterior, or exoskeleton, which protects the body and is divided into several segments; even their long antennae are protected. The Spiny Lobster does not have claws but there are sharp spines on the abdomen. (These can cut into the skin if they are carelessly handled.)

The adults of Ascidiacea or Sea Squirts are typical sea-bottom dwellers. The photograph (facing page) is of a species of Halocynthia. The Sea Squirts live attached to rocks. Like so many other marine species, their larvae are very different from the adult animal; they have tails and are able to move freely. After metamorphosis, they become attached to the sea-bed, lose their tails and assume their adult shape. Sea Squirts are shaped rather like wine bottles, with two opposite holes – the oral hole through which the water containing food is drawn and the other hole which is used for excretion. Sea Squirts can vary in size from one centimetre to tens of centimetres. They are found in every ocean. Those species which live in cold waters are larger than species found in warmer seas. Although some live at a great depth, the majority are to be found within five hundred metres. Essentially, they are sedentary animals which feed on the micro-organisms in the seawater.

Below right: *Sponges are animals, although this fact was disputed for many years. Most sponges are irregular, both in shape and size. They have an internal spiny structure (spicules) of limestone or silica. They can be found in great numbers from tidal zones to the great* depths, *although they mostly live in deeper waters. They often live in association with other animal or plant organisms – some single-cell algae enter the sponge hole and provide the sponge with oxygen and organic substances.*

Like the Sea Anemone, the Anthozoans have long cylindrical bodies often enveloped in a mud-encrusted mucus. Their tentacles are arranged in two concentric circles; those on the outside are longer than the internal tentacles which grow inside the mouth. The species illustrated (right) is Cerianthus membranaceus; it is widespread in the Mediterranean and has green or violet tentacles which may grow to a length of thirty centimetres. Only its tentacles protrude from the sea-bed. It adapts very well to living in an aquarium and it can survive many years.

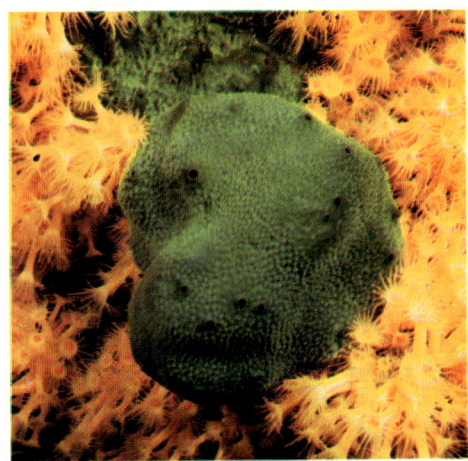

The Open Sea and the Ocean Depths

Left: *Like many other sea-birds, the albatross spends nearly the whole of its life on the open sea, only returning to land to breed. It feeds on fish and squid which it plucks from the surface waters. At the base of its beak are special glands which secrete the excess salt taken in with its diet. The excretion of surplus salt is common to many sea-birds which take in far more than they need; the excess is passed out via the nostrils.*

Life is present everywhere in the open sea, from the surface waters down to the abyssal (greatest) depths, even in the deepest ocean trenches, sixteen to seventeen kilometres beneath the surface. However, life-forms are less abundant at the ocean surface than in coastal waters. This is because the surface water of the open sea (which has most of the factors necessary for plant growth, with abundant sunshine) is poor in mineral salts and contains very little of the mineral substances vital for plants. On the other hand, the deepest waters are rich in mineral salts, although here the absence of sunlight precludes photosynthesis — the photochemical process by which green plants change inorganic substances into organic matter. Therefore, in both environments, plant-life, the first link in every food-chain, is very limited and this limitation restricts the development of animal life. There are exceptions to this rule; in some ocean regions rising currents carry nutritious substances to the sunlit surface waters, encouraging the growth of marine plants and therefore of marine animals.

Below: *In the absence of any shelter or hiding-place in the open sea, anchovies gather in large compact shoals, seeking protection from predators. Although some are eaten, many will escape.*

Below: *The Sargasso Sea gets its name from the sargassum seaweed, an alga with tiny air bladders which allow it to float. The Sargasso Sea is a relatively calm area in the Atlantic Ocean where algae carried by currents from the American coast build up and float in masses giving the appearance of a field of sargassum.*

Life in the Open Sea

Those animals which live in the open sea have had to adapt to its conditions, particularly in methods of self-defence. Many, such as the tunny and the cuttlefish, rely on speed; others such as the anchovy and sardine, gather in great shoals. Flying-fish and certain species of cuttlefish are even capable of projecting themselves above the water's surface and covering several metres in this way. Many invertebrates such as the Arrow Worm, *Sagitta setosa* and the salps have completely colourless and transparent bodies, which not only make them invisible to their predators but also make it easier for them to hunt their own prey.

Animals of the open sea have also had to overcome the problem of remaining buoyant for long periods. Some of the smaller species solve this by

Sharks are the most voracious of the large sea-animals. They threaten everything that swims. Some of the larger sharks are a serious hazard to man. Their mouths are full of sharp teeth and their skin, similar in texture to sandpaper, is dotted with small denticles or spines and can be used like sandpaper.

attaching themselves to larger fish. Whales, for instance, provide a home for suckerfish, algae, barnacles, copepods and many other small crustaceans. Some gastropods have evolved an unique method to keep themselves buoyant. They counteract the weight of their shells by making a kind of raft out of mucus bubbles. Attached to this, upside down, they are carried along by the currents. The minute life-forms which make up plankton use tiny bristles, lateral expansions like wings, or drops of oily liquid to maintain their buoyancy.

In the Abyssal Depths

Sunlight diminishes as depth increases, until it disappears entirely. In the darkness of the abyss, food is scarce and there is a total lack of vegetation. Many small fish and invertebrates rise to the surface in search of food. Others eat animal-and plant-debris which sinks from the upper waters. They, in their turn, provide nourishment for other larger animals and, in this way, start the food-chain of the abyssal depths.

The cold is particularly intense in this environment since heat is unable to penetrate this far down. Consequently, the animals living here have a very low body-temperature and grow only very slowly, within an overall slow life rhythm. Pressure increases with depth: at 1,000 metres it is already 105 kilograms per cm^2; at 10,000 metres it is more than a tonne.

Teleostei or Bony Fish

Red Mullet

Tunny

John Dory

Plaice

Hake

Angler Fish

The important characteristics of all bony fish is the presence of a partially or entirely ossified bony skeleton. Ninety-five per cent of the 26,000 known species of fish belong to this category. Most have a streamlined shape to reduce water resistance. Swordfish are among the fastest of the bony fish, believed to be capable of 100 k.p.h. Other fast-swimming bony fish are flying-fish which can cover more than fifty metres in one leap, and the tunny whose bursts of speed reach 70 k.p.h.

Virtually all bony fish have a swim-bladder; by regulating the contents of this organ a fish can adjust its specific gravity to the surrounding water pressure and rise vertically to the surface without using its fins. Bony fish are found in both salt and fresh water. The Red Sturgeon is the largest species of bony fish, growing to a length of eight metres and weighing more than a tonne. The smallest is a species of goby found in the Philippines; this is also the smallest of all the vertebrates — the female is only eleven millimetres long and weighs six grams.

There are two basic types of eggs produced by fish: 1) pelagic — containing a drop of oil which enables them to float on the surface among the plankton. 2) demersal — those which sink to the bottom, having a

Barracuda

Swordfish

Small Flying Fish

specific gravity greater than that of
the water in which they are deposited.
Some species lay thousands of eggs
but relatively few survive the countless dangers present in the ocean.

Invertebrates

The sea contains innumerable invertebrates; many of them can be seen in
the inter-tidal zone.
These include sponges, Sea Anemones
and coral. Although they vary in
shape and colour, they are funda-
mentally of a similar and very primitive basic structure, consisting of two
cellular layers (one internal and the
other external) separated by a gelatinous substance. Other animals higher
up the evolutionary scale have more
complex structures. These include
the many types of segmented crustaceans (crayfish, Spiny Lobster, crab,
krill) which play an important role in
many marine food-chains.
Some crustaceans are of considerable
size. The Giant Crab, found in Japan,
measures four metres with its claws
extended. Other invertebrates include
many molluscs (such as mussels,
oysters, cuttlefish and octopus)
characterized by a soft body and a
shell which is sometimes not visible
— as in the case of the cuttlefish and
octopus. Even the famous cuttlefish
bone is not a bone at all but a layer of
shell.

Cod

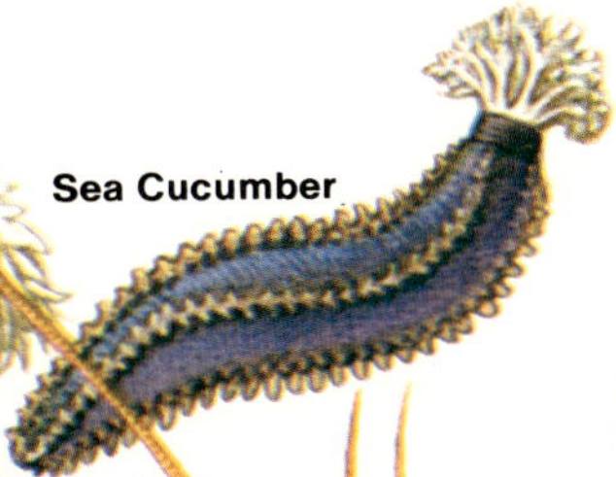

Sea Cucumber

Pearly Nautilus

**Hermit Crab
with Sea
Anemone**

Lobster

Cartilaginous Fish

Basking Shark

Tiger Shark

Lesser Spotted Dogfish

Tope

Hammerhead Shark

Monkfish or Angel Fish

In contrast to the bony fish, Chondrichthyes or cartilaginous fish have skeletons composed entirely of cartilage. There are three types: shark form; ray form (rays and mantas); and the Chimera or Rabbit Fish — a small group with both bony *and* cartilaginous characteristics. Cartilaginous fish have very rough skin, like sandpaper in texture, because of the tough scales covering it. The ray's scales have undergone many changes in the process of evolution; on the back and tail they have been modified into tough spines or thorns. Cartilaginous fish are found in the open sea where they are forced to swim continuously as, without a swim-bladder, they would otherwise sink to the bottom. Sharks (Selachii) are generally excellent, rapid swimmers, propelling themselves by undulating their bodies and strong tails. Some of the Selachiians can swim even faster; by expelling water through their gills they achieve a form of water-jet propulsion. Because of their flat bodies, rays and mantas have a swimming movement similar to that of a bird in flight — rhythmically undulating their large lateral fins. Although their vision is poor, Chondrichthyes have a highly-developed sense of smell which guides them unerringly in their search for food.

Giant Shark

White Shark
(with Pilot Fish)

Remora (Sucker Fish)

Blue Shark

Thresher

Porbeagle

Sandshark

Spiny Ray

Fertilization occurs internally in all Chondrichthyes. Males have the pelvic fins modified to form claspers which assist during fertilization.

Reproduction occurs in different ways. Some species, such as the Thornback Ray and the Lesser Spotted Dogfish, lay flattish (almost irregular) eggs, protected by a horny sheath. In other species, the young develop in the eggs which are retained within the mother's oviducts. Even after hatching they remain inside the mother fish for a short while before birth.

The cartilaginous fish of the open sea (such as sharks and mantas) are viviparous — they give birth to living young. The young of some species of shark show early signs of aggression when still in the mother's womb; in fact, the larger "babies" eat their smaller brothers.

All cartilaginous fish are carnivorous. Their prey ranges from plankton to very large animals.

The Great White Shark is one of the most feared species; it would not hesitate to follow a ship right up to the coast, attacking everything that moved.

Almost as dangerous are the Tiger Sharks found in the coastal waters of the warmer seas and the Blue Shark which never leaves the open sea.

The Abyssal Depths

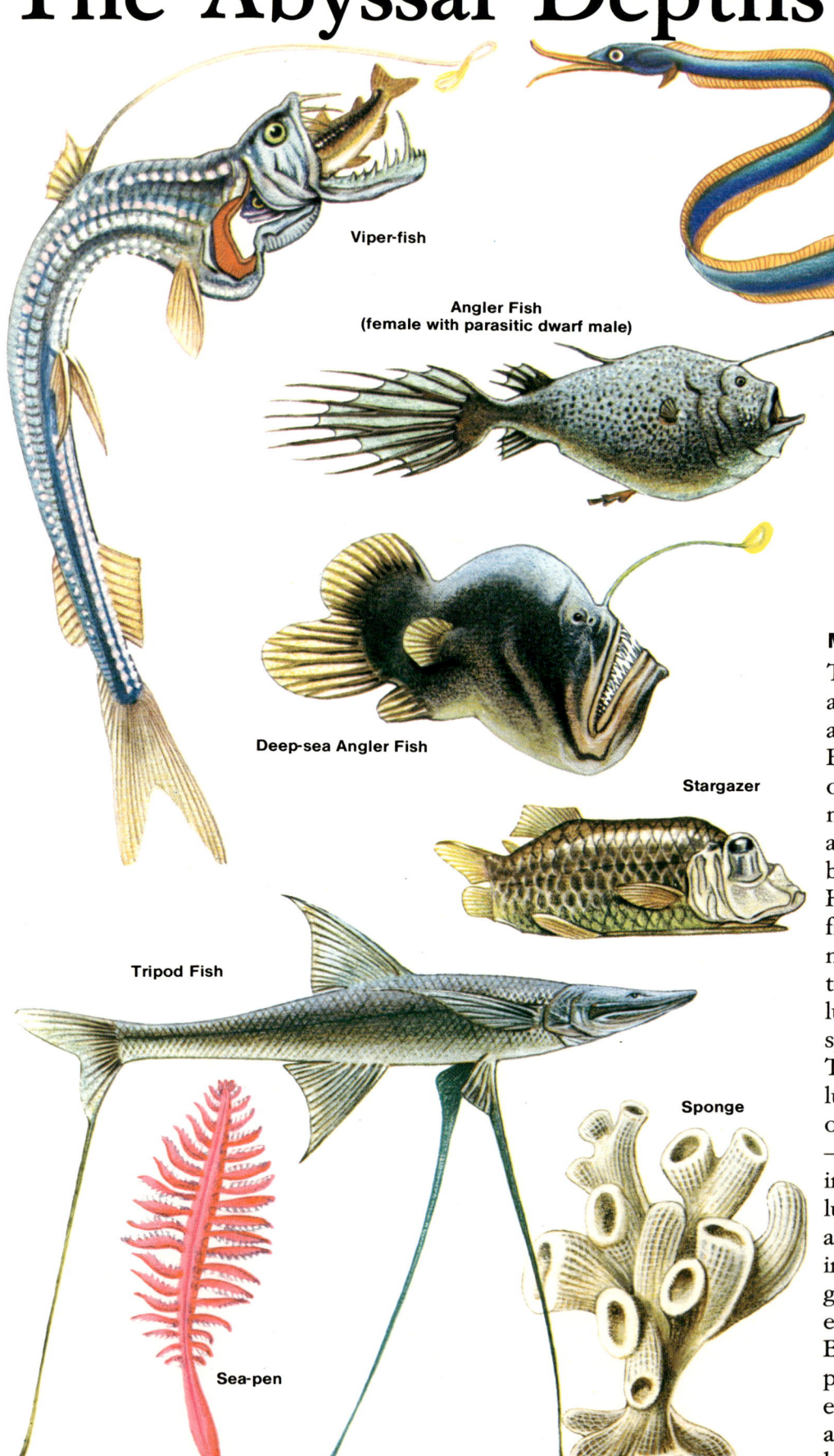

Spiny Eel

Viper-fish

Angler Fish
(female with parasitic dwarf male)

Deep-sea Angler Fish

Stargazer

Tripod Fish

Sponge

Sea-pen

Monsters of the Deep

The fish found in the abyssal depths are usually small and often hideous in appearance.

Because light is absent (the sun's rays only penetrate to a depth of 240 metres), colouring is usually black and brown, occasionally relieved by bright red fins as in the case of some Holocentrids (Squirrel Fish) — small fish only a few centimetres long. As a means of mutual identification in the total darkness, some species emit luminous signals using luminous spots, formed by light-producing cells. This phenomenon is known as bio-luminescence or living light and occures when a particular substance — luciferin — combines with oxygen in the presence of an enzyme called luciferase. A series of chemical re-actions takes place to produce energy in the form of a cold light, usually green and blue although occasionally even yellow or red.

Bioluminescence also serves to attract prey. The Abyssal Angler Fish, for example, has luminous filaments above and below its mouth which lure fish that feed on tiny luminous

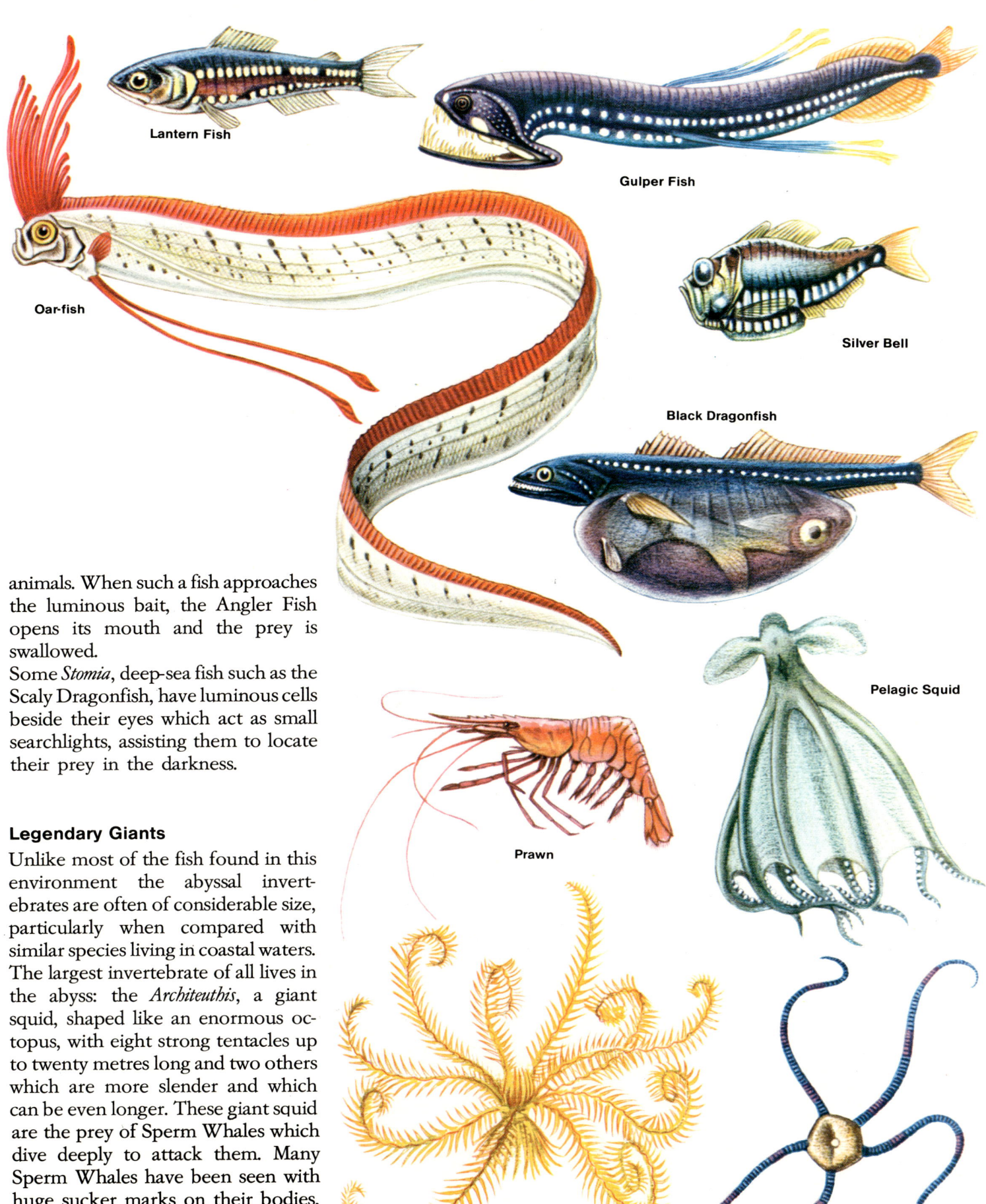

Lantern Fish

Gulper Fish

Oar-fish

Silver Bell

Black Dragonfish

Pelagic Squid

Prawn

Feather Star

Brittle Star

animals. When such a fish approaches the luminous bait, the Angler Fish opens its mouth and the prey is swallowed.

Some *Stomia*, deep-sea fish such as the Scaly Dragonfish, have luminous cells beside their eyes which act as small searchlights, assisting them to locate their prey in the darkness.

Legendary Giants

Unlike most of the fish found in this environment the abyssal invertebrates are often of considerable size, particularly when compared with similar species living in coastal waters. The largest invertebrate of all lives in the abyss: the *Architeuthis*, a giant squid, shaped like an enormous octopus, with eight strong tentacles up to twenty metres long and two others which are more slender and which can be even longer. These giant squid are the prey of Sperm Whales which dive deeply to attack them. Many Sperm Whales have been seen with huge sucker marks on their bodies, showing signs of a battle with these monsters of the deep.

The Birth of an Atoll

Red coral forms fairly sparse colonies, strengthened by a rigid and calcareous skeleton which is pink in colour. Inside it live the white coral polyps. In addition to the normal polyps, which can feed and reproduce, there are other much smaller types of simple structure which are able to contract. These promote the circulation of water inside the calcareous tube. Some filamentary algae live in the coral formation, symbiotically with the coral, having adapted to living in almost total darkness. They receive protection against predators and they rid the coral of the carbon dioxide produced during its normal respiration. This carbon dioxide would otherwise damage the coral, since it affects the production of the limestone of which the coral's stony skeleton is composed.

The Crown of Thorns, a species of starfish, has assumed an importance or even notoriety in recent decades. Some undetermined change in factors which formerly restricted it have brought about vast increases in its numbers. These starfish feed on coral polyps, – the living creatures which actually produce the coral. This has led to the destruction of first the polyps and then the coral reef, which, a living structure, cannot regenerate itself. Control of these starfish is further complicated by their extraordinary regenerative powers; if they are cut into pieces, the pieces regenerate into complete individuals.

An atoll is an island of coral, formed by a living animal. Roughly circular in shape, it is enclosed in a central lagoon, connected to the sea by one or more channels.

Several theories exist regarding the origin of atolls. One is that they were ancient coral-encircled islands which gradually sank below sea-level whilst the coral developed centrifugally in relation to the island. Another theory sees them as volcanic craters colonized in a ring formation by the corals. The most typical and numerous atolls are situated in the Laccadive and Maldive archipelagos of the Indian Ocean and in the Caroline and Fiji archipelagos of the Pacific Ocean. In these regions the water is oxygenated and its temperature varies between 20°C and 30°C. Reef-building corals require warm, shallow water with very little suspended mud and must not be exposed to the sun or rain for long. The coral animal is a small polyp (a coelenterate like a miniature Sea Anemone) which secretes the stony matter which forms the basis of coral.

Coral reefs form atolls. They thrive best in warm, well-oxygenated and well-lit waters, where salinity is rather high, and where currents frequently renew the water. They do not form where the temperature is below 18°C. The ideal temperature for them is between 20° and 30°C. The lumps of coral we see out of water are the dead skeletons of thousands of tiny coral polyps.

An aerial view of a coral island. Particularly noteworthy are the rounded shape and the centrifugal expansion of the coral colonies towards the open sea. Each bit of living coral is covered with the daisy-like polyps whose small tentacles, like those of a Sea-Anemone, collect its food.

The Horny Coral Sea Fan is a strikingly beautiful type of coral. Unlike Red Coral it lives in colonies which are anchored to sand with a contractile stalk which allows a limited mobility.

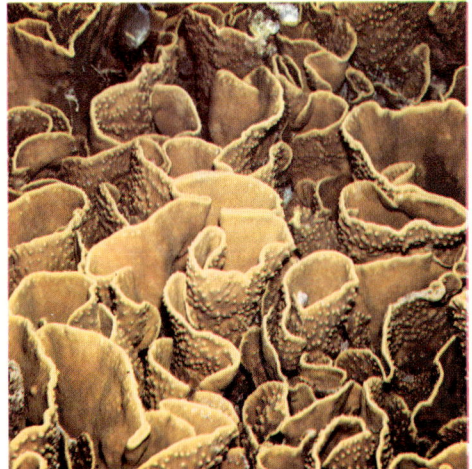

Life among the Coral

Coral reefs, rich in animal- and plant-life, make up a complicated eco-system which has been more or less stable for a long time. Their life-forms have developed intricate relationships with each other, facilitating the maximum exploitation of environmental resources. This arrangement creates a mutually advantageous symbiosis — two creatures (or a plant and animal) live together in mutual harmony with advantages for each. Many such associations exist in the coral reef; even the dead part of the reef provides shelter for many animals.

Above: The cowfish or trunkfish, Lactoria cornuta *is a typical tropical fish with its unusual appearance and beautiful colouring. The long "horns" on its head, prominent mouth and the somewhat square shape of its body, all help it to blend into the uneven and multi-coloured bed of the coral reef.*

Facing page: Characteristic of the coral-reef dwellers, the Butterfly Fish (of which there are many species). They are unusually-shaped and colourful, compressed laterally and with prominent lips. The photograph shows one of the species of Chaetodon, *recognizable by the absence from the lower edge of the operculum of the strong spine present in other members of the family.*

This tiny, graceful member of the Squirrel Fish family, Holocentridae, is widespread in South-East Asia. It remains hidden by day in the labyrinthine coral, coming out only at night to search for food.

Left: The Rainbow Fish (seen here feeding on the polyps of a coral) belongs to the wrasse family (Labridae), a name given to the family because all the various species have more or less prominent lips. (Latin labra = *lips). They are carnivorous and have very long dorsal fins and some spine-like rays. The tail-fin is square-shaped. Colouring, always vivid, differs considerably from one fish to another.*

The Art of Camouflage

The octopus is a cephalopod with eight tentacles and one of the largest heads of all the invertebrates. It belongs to the Phylum Mollusca, which includes snails, slugs, limpets and many others. An expert in camouflage, the octopus can change colour rapidly to adapt to the many colours of its own natural habitat. When under attack, it emits an inky cloud in which it hides from the aggressor. Its worst natural enemy is the Moray Eel. Left: An octopus swimming. Below: Another octopus well camouflaged in its shelter.

False eyes, sudden colour changes and screening clouds of ink all help to deceive predators. Camouflage is important to all animals, both prey and predator. For this reason many fish have, during their evolution, been modified to match their surroundings. For example, fish which live in the open sea, whether they are large or small, have dark uppersides to make them difficult to see from above, pale-coloured undersides so that when they are seen from below they blend with the sunlit waters above.

However, it is among the creatures which inhabit the coastal waters, particularly the corals, that camouflage is most effective. Here, animals often have bodies which are unusually-shaped and multi-coloured, with many marks and irregularities serving to break up the outline of their bodies. Out of their normal habitat, these fish seem very conspicuous or even grotesque in come cases; against their natural background in the coral reef, they are virtually invisible.

A Misleading Appearance

Coral-reef fish have other methods of camouflage, too. Some have very prominent markings shaped like eyes (usually on the tail), whilst their real eyes are well disguised by other markings and irregularities. In this way they can confuse predators about the direction in which they will try to escape.

Changing Appearance

Many fish change colour as a means of defence: the Left-eyed Flatfish, a group similar to the sole, take on a darker appearance similar to the colour of the sandy bottom into which they lightly burrow. Other species which are brightly-coloured by day, take on a more opaque and dull appearance at night.

All this is only possible because of the presence in the skin of special cells — chromatophores — some containing black, brown or grey pigment and others containing yellow, red or orange substances. A complex nervous-system permits the expansion or contraction of all these cells, creating the colour changes. A tropical sea-perch or grouper can assume eight colour variations, either uniform or striped.

A Marine Porcupine

Shape as well as colour is important in effective self-defence. When the Porcupine Fish feels threatened, it inflates its prickly body into an almost spherical shape to discourage any aggressor. Some crabs, on the other hand, are disguised by covering themselves with particles of algae or with shells. Predators also adopt strange positions to disguise themselves. The Trumpet Fish, for instance, takes a vertical position with its head downwards and sways on the bottom in an elongated form, imitating a seaweed and waiting for the tiny prey on which it feeds.

Snipe Fish which are small, slender fish, whose pale colour is broken by a dark longitudinal stripe, hide head downwards among the long prickles of Sea Urchins, and become virtually invisible here.

The Red Scorpion Fish is a rather ugly creature, with a large, spiny head and a very large mouth. It usually lives on the sandy bottom, at a depth of between 200 and 300 metres, where it blends well with its surroundings. Some species live near the shore. Their spines can sting if they puncture the skin and inject their paralyzing venom.

The Frog Fish captures its prey by fishing. It stays completely still on the sea-bed where it blends perfectly into the background and releases its fishing-line, – a projection which looks like a thin strand of seaweed. This attracts small fish to investigate and the Frog Fish seizes them.

The Stargazer is a fish which usually lives burrowed into the sand and extends only its worm-like tongue above the surface to attract its prey.

Animal Associations

Strange Alliances

The voluntary association of two animals, two plants, or a plant and an animal for mutual benefit is called symbiosis. It sometimes provides the exception to the marine rule: "eat or be eaten". A typical example is provided by the "Barber" Fish and his "clients". This tiny species of Labridae, or wrasse, feeds on the minute parasitic crustaceans which it finds on other fish. Before feeding, the Barber Fish performs a dance in front of the client so that it can be recognized; then it can approach in safety. Once the client or host fish has recognized the wrasse, it relaxes and allows itself to be cleaned of all its parasites. Even the Moray Eel appreciates this service. Some associations are not always to the benefit of both partners. In the case of the Pilot Fish which accompany sharks, the advantage is all on one side. These fish do not lead or guide the sharks (as was originally thought) but take advantage of the currents made by the sharks to travel at the same speed — a speed they could never achieve on their own. Sharks have to submit to another parasite, the *Remora* or Sucker Fish. This fish has a type of sucker on its head with which it attaches itself to the body of a large fish, most often a shark, to enable it to travel without effort. Sucker Fish, which are about ninety centimetres in length, have also been known to attach themselves to the keels of ships.

Below: Known also as the Sea Cucumber, the Holothurian is an unusual creature living on the sandy sea bed, partly burrowed. It has a crown of tentacles around its mouth and uses these to seize its prey. Inside its intestines the Fierasfer shelters and feeds. This is a small transparent, slender fish which lives in the Mediterranean. There are related species in the tropics. They live inside Sea Cucumbers, Sea Anemones and other sea creatures and they are protected by the host.

Above: A greatly enlarged photograph of the Clown Fish among the tentacles of the Sea Anemone. Below: Anemone or Clown fish provide a good example of symbiosis. These are small fish which shelter among the poisonous tentacles of the Sea Anemone without suffering any harm. This is because their bodies secrete a mucus which neutralizes the toxic effect of the tentacles. Both creatures benefit from this relationship. The tiny fish may well attract others to investigate and these will be caught by the sting and tentacles of the Sea Anemone.

Facing page: Unlike other crustaceans the Hermit Crab has no shell of its own. It protects its soft abdomen by squeezing itself into the shells of dead gastropods. This ingenious animal will improve its defensive system by living with a Sea-Anemone on the shell. From this position the Sea-Anemone discourages potential aggressors with its tentacles. The Sea-Anemone is able to feed on bits torn from the prey by the voracious Hermit Crab. It gets food and transport and gives the crab protection and camouflage.

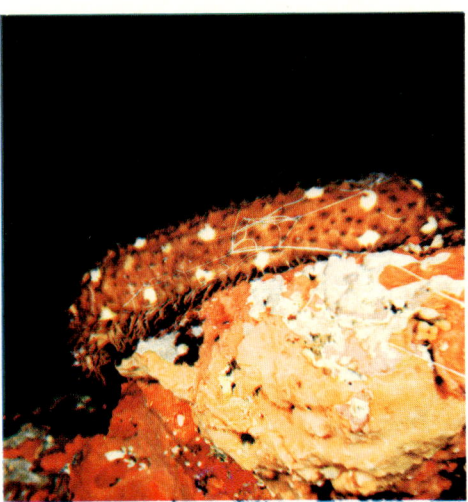

Dangers of the Sea

Jelly fish are easily reconized by their transparent umbrella-shaped bodies. They float along with the currents and use their tentacles to trap their prey. In their attacks they may also excrete a toxic fluid which, in some tropical species, is lethal to Man.

Weever Fish is common on the shores of the Mediterranean and on the Atlantic coasts from Norway to West Africa. During the day, these fish tend to bury themselves in the sand with just the top of their noses protruding. They snap up any passing small fish or shrimps. Each of the gill covers and the dorsal fin have poisonous spines which, in contact with bare feet, are very painful but not deadly. Many other fish, both coastal and deep-sea, have poisonous spines; some of them can cause severe poisoning if handled carelessly and some are deadly to Man. Other fish, such as the Trigger Fish, have toxic flesh. Usually these dangerous animals, like their insect and reptile counterparts, have very conspicuous colourings to warn possible predators that it is better to avoid them.

Hidden Weapons

The several species of sting-ray have poisonous tail stings. In the largest species the tail can be forty centimetres long. Most of these fish keep to shallow coastal waters and some even enter the estuaries of major tropical rivers. When they are threatened, the sting-rays lash out violently with their spiny tails causing deep lacerations and poisoning with their venom.

Even brightly-coloured, seemingly harmless Dragon Fish and Surgeon Fish have hidden weapons — very sharp spines which discourage even the most tenacious of predators.

Portuguese Man o' War

One of the most dangerous creatures

Poisons

Stinging cells, toxic flesh and electric shocks are often hidden in brightly-coloured and graceful-looking animals. Camouflage not only helps the hunted species by enabling it to blend into the background; it can also be used as a snare by the hunter. If the hunter is well camouflaged the unsuspecting prey does not see it until it is too late. Many coastal fish have spines, some of which cause only pain if trodden on by a barefoot bather; others contain dangerous toxins. The

found in warm and temperate seas resembles a galleon in full sail when it is fully inflated. Hence it is known as the Portuguese Man o' War. It consists of a bladder full of air called a pneumatophore, below which are many trailing tentacles, up to twelve metres long in larger species. These tentacles have countless stinging cells on them and these cells contain a poison as potent as that of the cobra. When the sea becomes rough the Man o' War deflates its air-bladder and sinks below the disturbed surface. As soon as the sea becomes calm again, the bladder is reflated by a gas produced by a special gland and the jelly-fish floats to the upper waters. It feeds on any marine animal which has the misfortune to be trapped in its tentacles.

Right: *The Moray Eel. Its bite is very painful and dangerous. The mucus of its palate secretes a poisonous liquid which is injected by biting.*

Right: *The Electric Ray has a very special method of defence and attack. Its body contains two large electric organs capable of generating violent shocks, in some species exceeding 200 volts and 2000 watts power.*

Below: *A member of the Scorpion Fish family like the Stone Fish, the Dragon Fish lives in the coral reef. At the base of each of the spines of its dorsal fin it has spines connected to glands which secrete a toxic poison.*

Marine Reptiles

A Green Turtle. This is a large marine turtle, up to 1.2 metres long and weighing more than 450 kilograms. These reptiles are well adapted to their aquatic environment. Their flat, paddlelike flippers making them excellent swimmers. They spend almost their entire lives in the open sea: the female only comes ashore to lay her eggs. They cannot move as easily on land as they do in the water and the female has great difficulty dragging herself along the beach, almost suffocating from her own weight. She digs a hole in the sand, into which she deposits up to one hundred eggs, and then returns to the sea. In about eight weeks the young turtles emerge from the eggs and, guided by instinct, make straight for the sea. Many dangers face them on this short journey. Crabs, gulls and sea-eagles attack them. Only a very small proportion reach the comparative safety of the water.

Only Partly Aquatic

Marine reptiles are not completely adapted to an aquatic environment because they are only able to breathe at the surface of the water and cannot extract oxygen from water as fish can. Their distribution is limited almost entirely to tropical and sub-tropical seas and they include many species of snake, some turtles and a single marine lizard which is related to the land iguana.

Marine Turtles

The largest marine reptile is the Leathery Turtle, *Dermochelys coriacea*, which is over 1.2 metres long and

The marine iguana, Amblyrhynchus cristatus, is related to the land iguana. It is found only around the coasts of the Galapagos Islands. It is about 1.5 metres long with a dark scaly skin. It is well adapted to water and is a good swimmer. It goes into the sea to hide at the slightest sign of danger. When resting on the shore, it never travels more than about fifteen metres from the water's edge. It mostly feeds on an alga which grows low-tide level.

weighs about 750 kilograms. It belongs to the turtle family and, unlike related species, it has a leathery skin instead of a horny scaled shell. It occurs in the sea round South America, Africa, northern Asia, North America and even occasionally on the coasts of Europe.

Some turtles are great travellers. The Green Turtle covers more than 3,500 kilometres in its migratory journey off the coast of Brazil. All turtles travel considerable distances in search of food, although no others can match the migration of the Green Turtle. There are two races, one in the Mediterranean and Atlantic and the other in the Indian and Pacific Oceans. This species is hunted because of its food value — it is used to make turtle soup.

Poisonous Snakes

There are some sixty known species of sea-snakes. They are related to the cobra and are found in the warm coastal waters of the Indian and Pacific Oceans. Although the least known of the marine reptiles, they are the most abundant. Some species grow to a length of three metres but the average is about 1.5 metres. They are all very poisonous and can be dangerous to Man although few fatalities occur. Two basic colour patterns are found on sea-snakes: an inconspicuous camouflaged type, pale below and dark above, similar to many fish; and a type ringed in black and grey green. They are both well protected by their venom.

In many species the body is compressed laterally to improve swimming abilities. The long tail is shaped like the blade of an oar and helps to propel the body through the water. These snakes have nostrils which close to allow them to stay submerged for a long time. The nostrils are situated very close to the apex of the muzzle so that the animal can lie just below the water's surface.

The Estuarine Crocodile is also known as the Salt-water Crocodile. It swims with great agility as far as the open sea, although coasts and estuaries are its normal habitat; it is not at all unusual to find this crocodile 100 kilometres up river. As they grow to a length of six metres and are very aggressive these reptiles can be dangerous to Man. In general, however, they attack only cattle and sheep. They occur on the coasts of India, and Sri Lanka, and throughout Indonesia and northern Australia. Little is known about their life history. They have been hunted so ruthlessly for their skins that they are now an endangered species. Steps are being taken to make this hunting illegal.

Marine snakes can remain submerged for more than six hours at a time, thanks to their large lungs. The lungs extend almost the whole length of the body and perform the same function for the snake as a fish's swim-bladder, helping to keep it afloat.

Nearly all species of marine snakes give birth to their young in the sea; the Amphibious Sea-snake is one of the very few which come ashore to lay their eggs.

Migration

Marine Migration

Natural instincts drive many animals to travel thousands of kilometres to reach a traditional breeding-ground. Migrations usually follow seasonal patterns, even in the sea. The animals leave one area to find the special environment they need for breeding and, although migration is more obvious on land, there are many marine animals which are migratory. Some examples are well-known, although still not fully understood. Eels, which leave the rivers of Europe to travel to the Sargasso Sea off Central America to breed, are probably the most famous. The return journey across the Atlantic is made by the young eels, which look so differ-

After spending eight to ten years in the rivers, Lakes, ponds and swamps of North America and Europe, eels begin their long one-way journey to their spawning-grounds in the Sargasso Sea. The females swim or are carried by the currents down-river to the river estuaries where they join the males. The eels eat voraciously at this time until they have a thick layer of fat under their skins on which they can live during the long sea journey. The migration takes several months and, on arriving in the warm waters of the Sargasso Sea, the females lay their eggs at depths of between 400 and 500 metres where they are fertilized by the males. The adults then die, exhausted by their long migration. On hatching, the larvae immediately set out to return to the regions from which their parents came. This journey takes up to three years as they drift across the Atlantic. Having reached their destination, the females swim up-river to fresh water and the males stay in the sea.

Illustrated here are the young stages of the eels and the routes of American and European eel larvae.

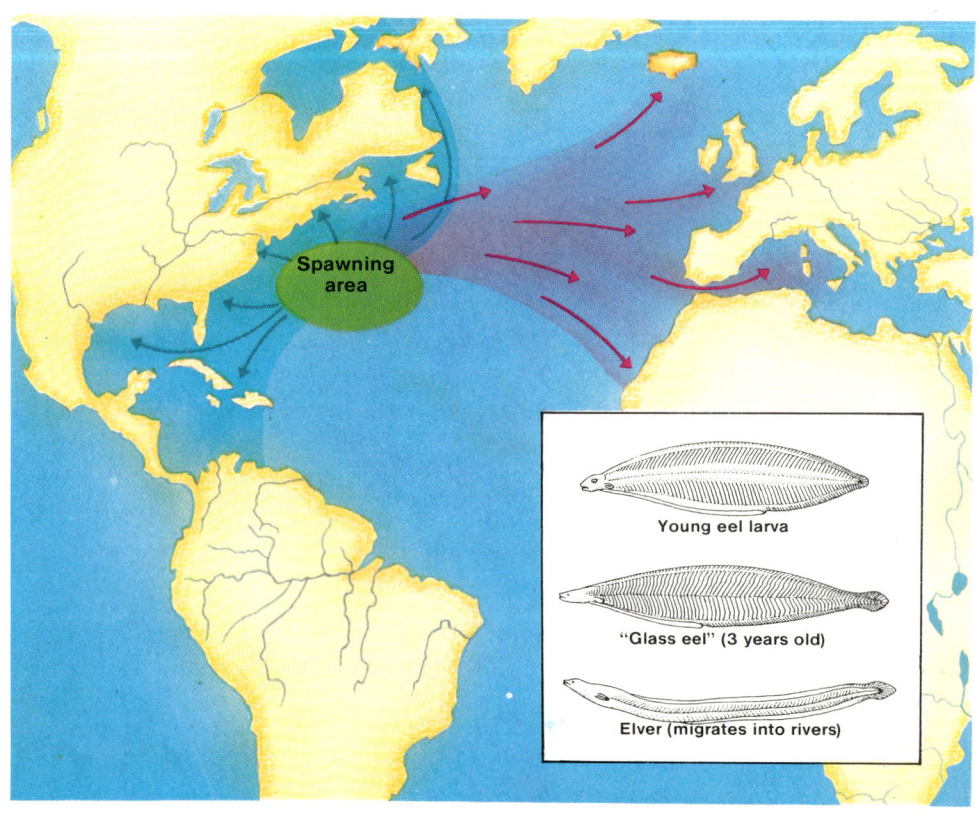

Spawning area

Young eel larva

"Glass eel" (3 years old)

Elver (migrates into rivers)

ent from the adults that they were formerly believed to be a different species. These young eels, between only five and ten millimetres long, are called Leptocephali and are carried across the Atlantic by the Gulf Stream. When they reach Europe they change into small white replicas of the adult eels and are called elvers. These then move up the rivers and mature into adults.

By contrast, salmon migrate from the sea to the rivers to spawn. Their migrations are famous. Fish such as mackerel swim in shoals along the European coast moving into deeper waters at the onset of winter. Marine turtles often migrate in small groups, unlike the huge shoals of mackerel, cuttlefish and herrings which make regular migratory movements. The invertebrates, including Crustacea and Mollusca, migrate from the coast to deeper waters at the breeding-season. Migration is triggered by many causes but, primarily, it is a response to changes in the environment — day length, temperature, etc. — and to changes in the body chemistry brought about by the action of the animals' hormones.

Migratory Marine Mammals

Some of the whales undertake spectacular journeys to their breeding-grounds. The Humpback Whale and Common Rorqual move from the Antarctic at the approach of winter. They travel northwards towards the tropics where their young are born. The Californian Grey Whale travels vast distances; in three months it moves from Mexico or California to the Bering Sea.

Any animal which feeds on the fish shoals must, of course, follow them if they migrate. Seals and sea-lions which spend most of their lives in the open sea migrate at certain times of the year to their breeding-grounds in the far north of the Pacific Ocean.

The Pacific salmon reaches maturity in the cold waters of the Alaskan Gulf. When they are between two and four years old the salmon leave this area (which is rich in food) and form groups which migrate to the breeding-areas. These extend from Alaska to California and from North Korea to Siberia. After a long and dangerous journey the salmon reach fresh water and stop feeding. They return to their own place of birth, fighting their way upstream against rapids and waterfalls. After the eggs have been laid and fertilized the adults die from exhaustion.

After a period which varies from one month to two years, the young salmon set off for the sea, and the cycle begins again.

Lakes

Lakes and pools are areas of standing water. They may be enormous, like Lake Victoria in central Africa, or they may be small ponds, either fairly permanent or very ephemeral. They may be salt-water or freshwater, or a combination of both which is called brackish. They are formed in many different ways. Geologically they can be basins hollowed out by the glaciers of the Ice Age, or they may form from a meandering river which cuts a new passage, leaving an ox-bow lake.

In the African rift valley, lakes were formed in a chain along the geological rift — Lake Tanganyika and Lake Malawi. Some almost circular lakes are formed in the craters of long extinct volcanoes. Over the world's land area there are vast numbers of lakes and ponds in different sizes and origins, with the non-marine ones all forming a habitat for freshwater animals and plants. Man is a great creator of artificial lakes, especially when dams are built for hydroelectric schemes, such as the lake at the Kariba dam. There are, of course, many smaller lakes, down to the garden ponds.

General Characteristics

Lakes may be in a variety of shapes and sizes. Depth depends very much on the lake's origin. A lake formed from a geological rift or scoured out in the Ice Age, such as Loch Ness, with a moraine (glacial debris) at the head of the valley, will be much deeper than a flooded valley or an ox-bow or horseshoe lake. Only about twenty of the world's lakes are deeper than 250 metres, the deepest being Lake Baikal (1,523 metres) and Lake Tanganyika (1,435 metres). Acoustic sounding equipment is used to determine the depth of lakes and also for the relief mapping of the lake bottom. From these measurements the total water content of a lake can be gauged. The study of the physical aspects of lakes has many applications. These include conservation and the use of water resources, whether for hydroelectric power, or irrigation, or directly as drinking water.

Even when the surface of a lake is calm and placid, the waters below are always moving. Differences in temperature can cause the water, which has a different density at different levels, to rise or fall or to flow gently along trying to reach equilibrium. Water is at its heaviest at 4°C. In a lake this water sinks to the bottom, while water at 6°C. may form a layer above it. The lake surface may freeze and this solid, but lighter, layer will stay at the top. Lakes which are fed by large rivers have different characteristics from those where the drainage is by seepage from the surrounding lands. The type of surroundings can have dramatic effects on the surface water. Long, narrow lakes in valleys can have the surface strongly affected by wind. All this helps to mix the chemicals which the water dissolves out of the rock or from the dead plants and animals in it.

Evaporation from the surface, especially in warm or windy weather,

Many algae flourish on the edges of lakes, creating an environment in which many animals live; single-cell protozoa, molluscs and aquatic insects as well as numerous species of fish including the voracious pike. Below: It waits, hidden in the vegetation and will attack anything that moves.

can remove a lot of water from a lake and cause movement within the lake. Finally, rain on the lake will add more fresh water to the system. Temperature changes in large lakes can be fairly gradual, but will be helped by strong winds whipping up the water.

The Evolution of Lakes

Geologically, most lakes exist only for a relatively short time. Lakes, even the large ones, may gradually fill up with accumulated silt and, unless there are strong currents, the lake will eventually disappear. A lake will last longer if it has a strong river flowing through it. However, relative to Man, many lakes are "permanent", even though formed only a few thousand years ago. Lakes themselves undergo changes over the years, passing through many phases. These phases fall generally into three categories: oligotrophic (promoting selective growth), eutrophic (promoting growth) and dystrophic (not favouring growth).

The young lake is subject to weathering and to wave action on the sides; minerals are brought in by small rivers and gradually the mineral content of the water increases. With this come the algae and other plant-life. As soon as the plant-life is there the animals follow and eutrophic conditions then exist. Some lakes seem almost permanently oligotrophic in rocky areas where there is little vegetation and the clear water is low in minerals. But eventually even these will develop into eutrophic lakes, with rich vegetation in the shallow water, and algae, fish and a host of small aquatic invertebrates in the deeper water. The photosynthetic action of the green vegetation helps to increase the organic substances in the lake and the vegetation spreads. Gradually there comes a time when there are more producers (plants) than consumers. When this eventually happens, a lake slowly becomes a marshy area. Man often accelerates this process, turning lakes into

Nearly all the great lakes of northern Italy are of glacial origin. The ice carved out valleys and basins and, as the ice melted, the waters filled the basins and formed lakes.

marshes and then draining them. Slow development of vegetation can be tolerated by lakes; they do not choke up overnight but continue the struggle between the spread of vegetation and the open water. If anything tips the balance in favour of the plants — for example, if extra organic matter is added, such as sewage or fertilizer — then the lake cannot always cope with the sudden rush of extra nutrients and the attendant rapid plant growth. The water gradually loses oxygen and a general decline will begin. Ultimately the vegetation dies and decomposes producing evil-smelling gases and masses of surface algae. Even large lakes can be killed and once they lose their natural oxygen they are difficult to revive.

Flora and Fauna of Lakes

Above: *The pike is a bony fish, up to 1.3 metres long. It is aggressive and has an insatiable appetite. It waits among the water-plants for its prey to come by, feeding not only on other fish but also on water-birds and small mammals like water voles. Like all predators, the pike is important in maintaining the biological balance of its environment, keeping down the numbers of the other species and preventing overcrowding.*

Below left: *The perch is a common freshwater fish throughout much of Europe. It breeds from March to June and lays thousands of eggs. Perch live in shoals and are mainly predatory. The perch is one of the freshwater fish sought by anglers.*

Below right: *Carp has been a popular source of food since ancient times. It occurs naturally in rivers and fresh water throughout the world and is now artificially bred in special ponds.*

The term lacustrine is used for both the flora and the fauna of lakes. In a final analysis the animal-life in the lake depends on the growth of the lake vegetation.

The plants on the shores range from those on drier ground to those whose roots and stems are submerged.

Further out, many free-floating species may occur. In smaller ponds they may completely blanket the surface, as does duckweed. There are also the totally submerged plants, many of which only show above the surface when they flower as, for example, Water Violet and Canadian Pondweed. Moss and innumerable algae can form large mats of green scum on the water surface.

The animals which live on the lake edge are far less varied than their marine counterparts.

In the shallow waters there are abundant insects, many of which are the young stages whose adults are aerial, such as the dragonflies.

Apart from fish, lake animals include small coelenterates (related to Sea Anemones) such as hydra, and planarians or flat worms.

Leeches occur in fresh water, and many snails, but never as many species as on the tidal seashore. There are also frogs and newts, the latter spending most of their lives in the water. Among the mammals there are otters, beavers, water-rats and, in Australia, the strange Duck-billed Platypus.

Further out, in the deeper water of the lake, fish, insects, crustaceans and other animals live. Above them, the water-birds fly.

Many species of birds build their nests near the lakeside, attracted by the abundance and variety of food to be found there. Each species has its own favourite habitat and its own specialized way of catching its food. Pelicans (above) often dive into the water with closed wings in pursuit of fish. Sometimes, swimming in groups, they herd the shoals of fish towards one particular point and then take turns to put their heads into the water and fill their large beaks with food. Waders, such as cranes and herons, wait in the shallower waters or on the banks for fish or frogs to come near. With only their long legs in the water, they spear their catch with their harpoon-like beaks. Flamingoes also stand in the water but they filter their food in minute particles from the water. Ducks, geese and swans have webbed feet to enable them to swim after the fish. The Barheaded Goose (right) like surface-feeding ducks, feeds on anything it can reach by submerging its neck and more than half its body in the water. Diving ducks, on the other hand, plunge to a depth of several metres to catch fish.

Rapids, Rivers and Estuaries

The Elephant's Trunk Snake is found in the rivers of India and Sri Lanka and in the Papuan islands. This lazy and harmless snake only rarely moves to dry land.

A river is a permanent watercourse, usually of a relatively constant nature, which runs in a bed. It has a regular, but not too steep, gradient. In this respect it differs from rapids which flow irregularly and slope steeply, restricting plant- and animal-life to a few highly-adapted species. Rivers are fed by melting snow and ice, by springs, streams, lakes and their tributaries. A river may be a tributary of another river, or of a lake, or it may flow directly into the sea.

The mouth of a river is called an estuary when it opens directly into the sea, or a delta when it breaks up into many small streams, each of which fans out to find its own way to the sea, forming a shape like the Greek letter delta. As the river flows towards the sea in the estuary the tidal effect can be seen and the mixing of sea water and fresh water produces differing conditions, gradually changing from fresh, through varying concentrations of saltiness, to sea water.

River Mammals

There are very few mammals which spend all or even a large part of their lives in water, but there are two totally aquatic species which live in rivers – the Amazon Dolphin and the Ganges River Dolphin. In addition, there are many mammals which depend on water for their survival. Otters, water voles and water shrews are all excellent swimmers which hunt for their food in rivers and lakes. Two large water rodents, the coypu and the capybara, live in South America. The largest mammal found in fresh water is the hippopotamus

A species of Guppy. Many of the tropical freshwater fish are brightly-coloured. They are much sought after as aquarium fish because of their graceful shapes and beautiful colours.

The River Crayfish can exceed fifteen centimetres in length. It is nocturnal and prefers chalky waters where it shelters in holes or under stones. It feeds on dead animals, such as molluscs and tadpoles, as well as other decomposed matter.

The kingfisher is one of the inhabitants of the river bank. It hunts for fish, plunging into the water to catch them. In severe, icy weather it may be forced to hunt along the sea shores. The Common Kingfisher of Europe and Asia (right) occurs also in Africa, India and as far east as New Guinea and some of the Pacific Islands. This kingfisher nests in burrows in river banks. It may use an old burrow but will excavate its own, up to two metres long, if necessary. There are about ninety species of kingfisher in the world.

which has adapted in many ways to an aquatic environment. It swims very well and, as it can close its ears and nostrils, it can stay under water for several minutes at a time. Its eyes are positioned so that it can see out of the water by lifting only the top of its head above the surface.

River Reptiles

Several species of crocodiles, caymans and alligators live in tropical rivers. They are predatory and are often very large. The largest reptile of all is the anaconda, over eight metres long, which spends a lot of time in water. It hunts mammals, birds and young cayman. The anaconda is a South American snake which is related to the boa. It kills its prey in the same way as the boa, by constriction. Many species of turtles live in tropical and temperate fresh waters; they vary in size from the huge South American Arrau Turtles, nearly three-quarters of a metre long, to the tiny Painted Turtles of the Mississippi River.

The sturgeon (right) is found along the Mediterranean and Atlantic coasts, as well as in the rivers which flow into these seas. In Spring, at breeding-time, both males and females go up-river where the eggs are laid. Caviar is made from the salted eggs of the species found in the Black Sea and the Caspian Sea. Sturgeons usually grow to a length of three metres and sometimes reach six metres.

The Amazon Basin: An Inland Sea

Great shoals of the voracious and aggressive piranhas live in the River Amazon. They attack wounded or sick fish as well as eating the remains of any large mammals which fall into the water, stripping them to the bone within a few minutes. There are four species of piranha. They are rapid swimmers and have numerous sharp teeth.

The elegant freshwater Angel Fish (below) and the tiny Neon Tetras (facing page) are two species of freshwater fish from the Amazon which have become well-known as aquarium fish.

A Slow Majestic River

The river's name has an unusual origin. In 1500 a party of Spaniards, including Pizarro, arrived in South America. They were attacked by long-haired Indians. These were at first thought to be women and so were nicknamed "Amazons" and so gave a name to the river "River of the Amazons".

It is almost impossible to comprehend the vastness of the Amazon basin, which covers an area of more than seven million square kilometres. Water flows slowly down to the mouth of the river. Since the dry and rainy seasons occur at different times in the various regions of the Amazon, the nature of the main river changes very little. This great basin, crossed by countless rivers (some of which are more than 1,500 kilometres long) contains several different types of habitats: aquatic; marsh and swamps; seasonally flooded areas. Like a gigantic aquarium, the River Amazon contains very varied and unusual species such as the voracious ara-paima, the largest freshwater fish, weighing up to 135 kilograms, the infamous piranha, the colourful Neon Tetras and the elegant Angel Fish. The Electric Eel is another unusual species found in this region; it stuns its prey with high-voltage electric shocks. Along the river banks can be seen the alligator-like caymans, giant Arrau Turtles and the capybara, a large rodent, about a metre long and weighing fifty kilograms.

The 6,280-kilometre Amazon River is one of the rivers which flows into the Atlantic. It brings this ocean about eighteen per cent of all the fresh water on the Earth's surface. The greater part of the massive basin is in Brazil but it also extends to Bolivia, Peru, Ecuador, Colombia, Venezuela and the Guyanas. Near its mouth, the main river branches out into the ocean. The mud carried down by the river, in suspension, colours the sea yellow, like a yellow protruding tongue.

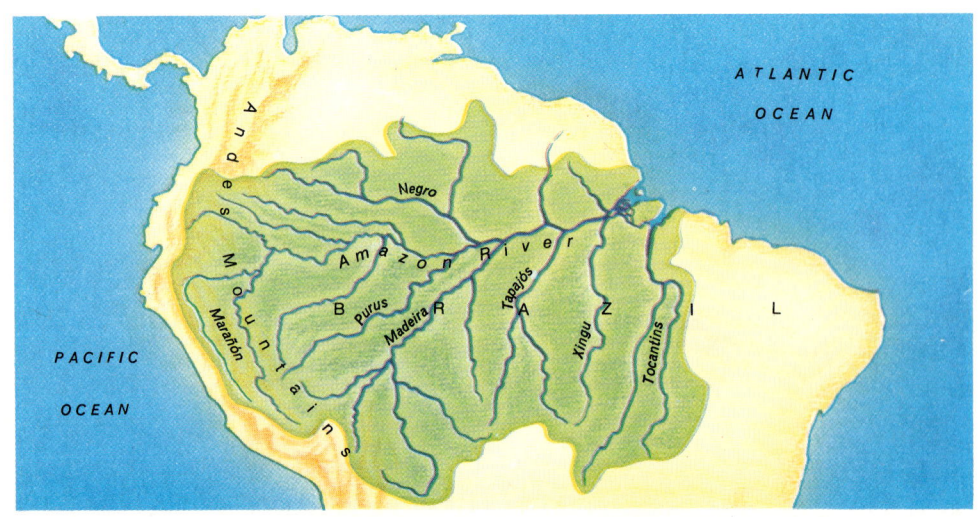

Fish and Invertebrates

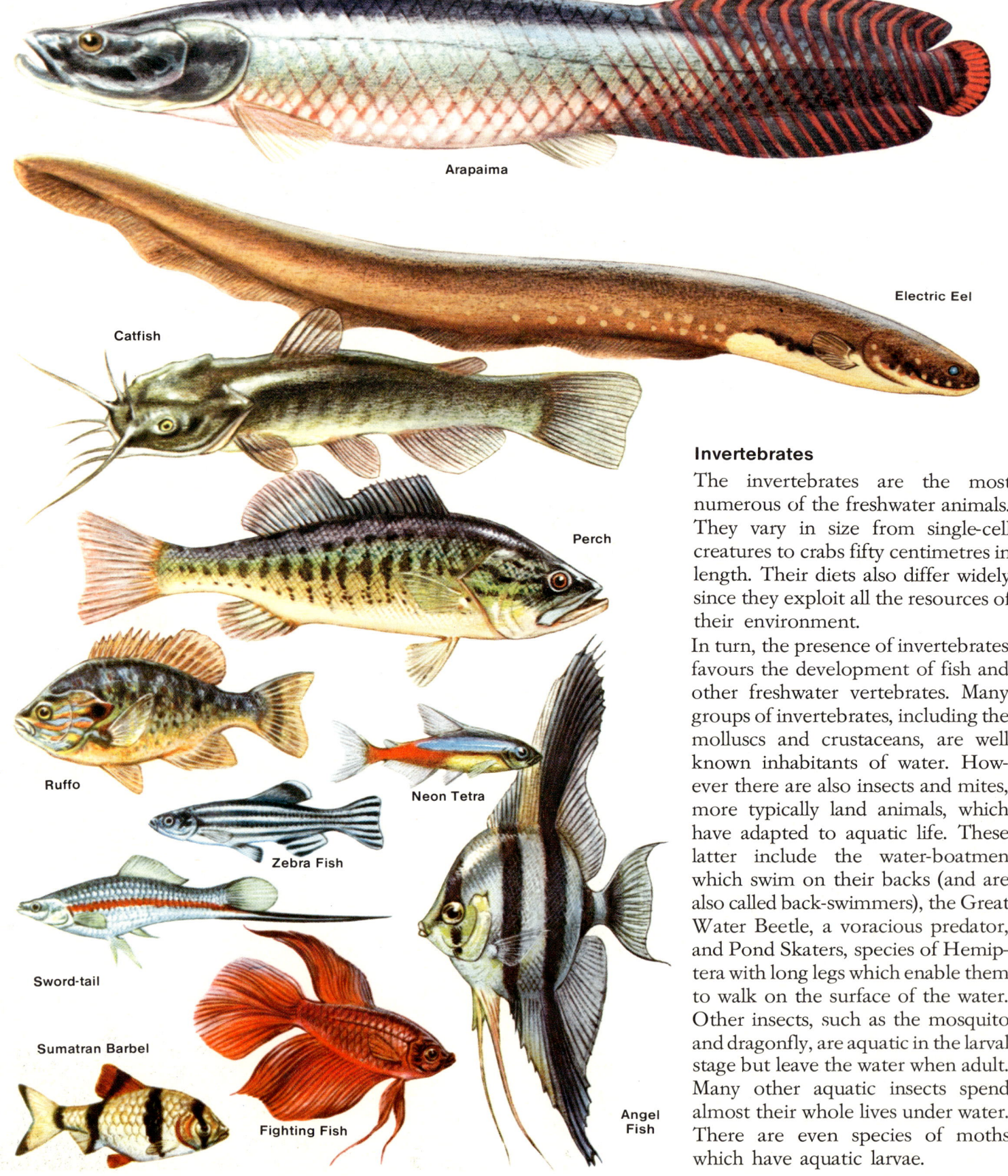

Arapaima

Electric Eel

Catfish

Perch

Ruffo

Neon Tetra

Zebra Fish

Sword-tail

Sumatran Barbel

Fighting Fish

Angel Fish

Invertebrates

The invertebrates are the most numerous of the freshwater animals. They vary in size from single-cell creatures to crabs fifty centimetres in length. Their diets also differ widely since they exploit all the resources of their environment.

In turn, the presence of invertebrates favours the development of fish and other freshwater vertebrates. Many groups of invertebrates, including the molluscs and crustaceans, are well known inhabitants of water. However there are also insects and mites, more typically land animals, which have adapted to aquatic life. These latter include the water-boatmen which swim on their backs (and are also called back-swimmers), the Great Water Beetle, a voracious predator, and Pond Skaters, species of Hemiptera with long legs which enable them to walk on the surface of the water. Other insects, such as the mosquito and dragonfly, are aquatic in the larval stage but leave the water when adult. Many other aquatic insects spend almost their whole lives under water. There are even species of moths which have aquatic larvae.

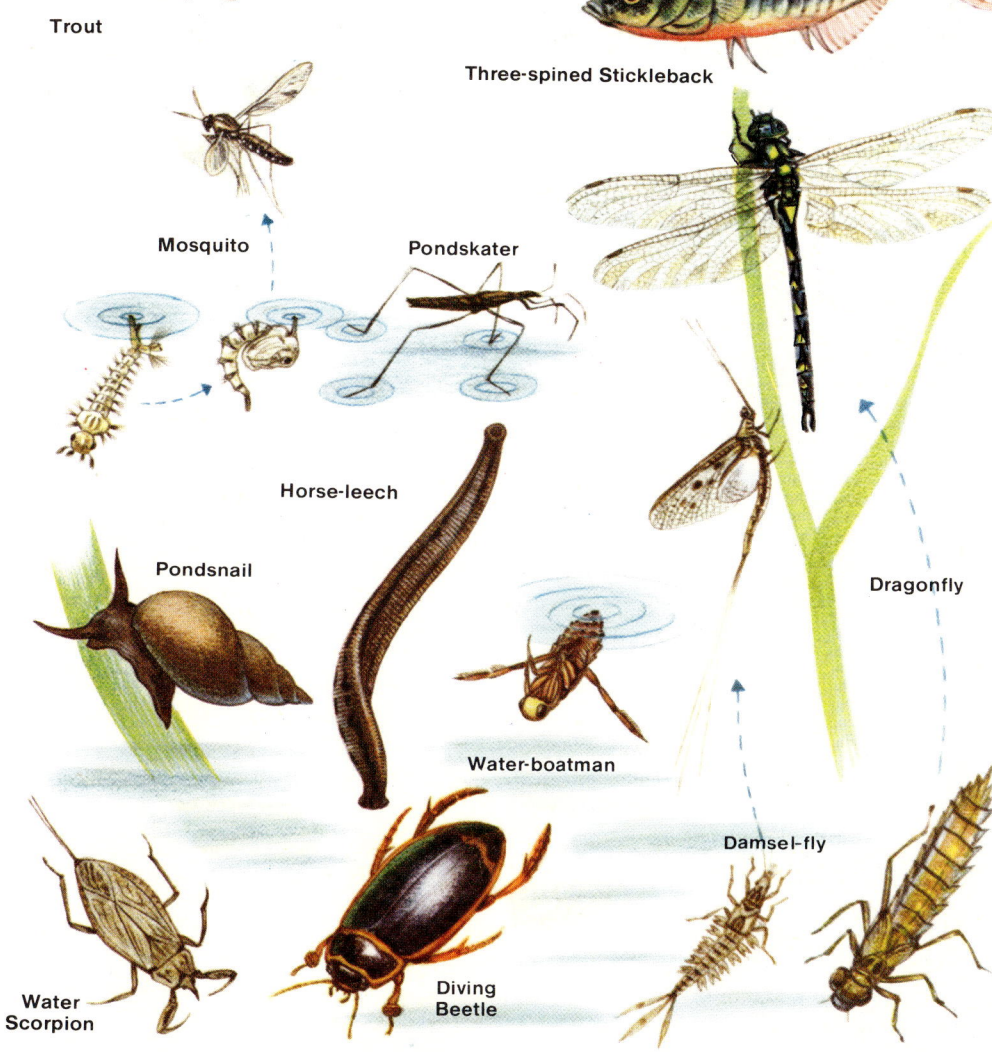

Tench

Mirror Carp

Barbel

Rudd

Trout

Three-spined Stickleback

Fish

About one third of all the known species of fish (over 25,000 species) live in fresh inland waters. Bony fish are the most numerous in species. A few species of ray and some sharks living in estuaries are the only cartilaginous fish to be found in these regions. The jawless fish are few in number and include the lamprey, a parasitical fish which feeds on the blood and flesh of other fish.

There are also the Lung Fish which can breathe air and survive out of water; they are found in Africa, South America and Australia. In the dry season these fish bury themselves in the river-bed or in a mound of mud where they may remain for two or three months.

As a result of the variety of food found in the rivers and lakes, the fish which live there have developed many different diets, so that there is enough food for all. Thus, as in all the other habitats, there are the herbivores (plant-eaters), the omnivorous fish (feeding on plants and animal matter) and the carnivores, such as the pike and piranha.

Mosquito

Pondskater

Horse-leech

Pondsnail

Water-boatman

Dragonfly

Damsel-fly

Water Scorpion

Diving Beetle

The Pond: A World in Itself

The Goliath Heron, found in Africa and India is about 1.5 metres tall. Its long neck and legs are well suited to its life in marshes where food is easily come by. It uses its beak and makes sharp stabbing thrusts with it to catch a variety of animals including fish, amphibians, crustaceans, insects, rodents and young birds.

The Water Crowfoot is a floating plant which has two types of leaves: (1) dissected, underwater ones; and (2) flat, typically leaf-like, floating on the surface. It is a perennial plant; in the autumn a small bulb full of starches is formed and this sinks to the bottom of the pond. In the Spring this bulb rises to the surface and the growth cycle starts once more.

In a pond the vegetation can be considered as forming a series of concentric circles, each with its different plants. First, the outer with marsh vegetation which prefers damp soil (where plants such as cotton-grass grow) but also with some plants growing in shallow water; second, the plants with roots in the bottom of the pond, almost totally immersed in water; third, the plants which are completely submerged.

The Origin of Ponds

A pond is a temporary mass of water of limited breadth and depth, whose bed is almost completely covered in vegetation. Far from being a stable system, it is transitional and eventually becomes dry grassland. A pond usually forms where a depression in the ground becomes filled with water brought by rain, melting snows or springs. However, it can also be caused by the burying of a lake by a river or erosion detritus. Ponds do not normally have an outlet, or exceed a depth of four or five metres.

The Environmental Factors

Pond water is usually stagnant, except when disturbed by wind, and it is subject to wide variations in both daily and seasonal temperature because of its shallowness. Water-levels fluctuate in the course of the year, depending on the wet and dry seasons. The light penetration is also very low; at a depth of two metres there is only fifteen per cent of the surface light. These factors, together with the chemical composition of the surrounding land, play a fundamental role in determining the animal and plant species to be found in a pond. Aquatic life in the smaller ponds is able to survive if the pond dries out, either by moving to another pond, as frogs and insects do, or by forming a protective stage, as the algae do, to wait for the pond to refill.

Facing page: *A pond in the Spring, showing the different types of vegetation.*

Pond-Life

Ponds are favourite collecting sites, attracting small children with jam-jars. The teeming life in a pond means that every scoop of the net brings out a mass of wriggling, squirming creatures which swim freely when dropped in the jar. Village ponds, the source of drinking water in the past, are now appreciated and preserved, not only as being aesthetically pleasing but also for ecological reasons. Pond-life is studied by most schools, being a readily available source of life which can be easily collected for the school aquarium. Frog-spawn is collected every year and, although not often successfully raised to the adult-frog stage, shows clearly the development of animal life from egg to active animal.

The Food-Chain

The rich greenness of ponds is usually due to the abundant algae in the water. In this the microscopic crustaceans, *Daphnia* and *Cyclops*, diminutive relatives of crabs and lobsters, find plenty of food. As well as these crustaceans and the related larger freshwater shrimps feeding on the algae, there are the abundant insects. Many of them (such as the larvae of some of the flies and caddisflies) are filter-feeders, straining off the minute plants and animals on which they feed. These are, in turn, fed on by the larger insects, water-beetles and dragonfly larvae which, in their turn, are eaten by frogs, newts, mammals and birds. Each step in the food-chain, or food-pyramid as it is also called, leads to a larger organism. Finally, the dead bodies and rotting vegetation at the bottom of the pond are decomposed by anaerobic (without air, — i.e. those living without oxygen) bacteria and fed on by the larvae of flies, and by bloodworms and other worms. All this provides the passage of energy from the water through the animals, finally returning to the pond for re-use in the cycle. Snails browsing over the vegetation scrape off some of the plant epidermis with their rasping organs, or radula, and they are eaten by birds and other animals.

Some plants are carnivorous: they trap tiny animals or other plants in special bladders where they are digested by enzymes and absorbed by the plants.

Many of these processes can be seen in an aquarium where pond-life can be more readily studied.

Left: The Ramshorn Snail, common in ponds and streams, is a mollusc with a thin, smooth shell, spiral and flattened in shape, from which it gets its name. It lives in marshy vegetation and lays its eggs in tiny masses stuck to submerged plants. There are several species ranging in size from a few millimetres up to thirty millimetres.

Right: There are a large number of species of water-boatmen. They include species popularly known as back-swimmers (Notonecta) which actually row themselves through the water in an upside-down position. Other water-boatmen (Corixa and related genera) swim with their backs upwards. They are hemipterous insects with sucking mouthparts. Notonecta is predatory and feeds on tadpoles and small fish, holding the prey in its forelegs while the body fluids are sucked out. Corixids are mainly vegetarians. Water-boatmen are strong fliers and migrate from pond to pond, mainly at night.

Above: The Damselfly (shown mating). They lay their eggs either on aquatic plants or directly into the water. After about one month a larva emerges from each egg, looking very different from the adult insect. In the course of its development in the water it goes through several stages, moulting its outer skin. Finally, it climbs up the stem of a plant out of the water. There, the skin splits releasing a fully-formed adult insect. The larva breathes the oxygen in the water through gills, whereas the adult breathes air.

Below: The Great Water Beetle is a tireless predator of small fish, amphibians and other insects. This beetle is not wholly adapted to an underwater life and it has to come to the surface periodically to breathe. To do this, it raises its abdomen, gently lifting the elytra to take in air underneath. The air then passes through special holes or spiracles into the insect's respiratory system which consists of a series of tubes or trachea. The beetle stores a certain amount of air between the elytra and the abdomen to prolong its underwater activities.

Below: The Water Scorpion, Nepa, is related to the water-boatmen; both are in the family Hemiptera. The long "tail" of the Water Scorpion is a breathing-tube which is protruded above the water surface, to take in air. The Water Scorpion walks slowly on the bottom or on aquatic plants, waiting for its prey. Its fore-legs are modified like pincers and it seizes its prey with them. Holding the victim's body firmly, the Water Scorpion pierces it with its tubular rostrum or "beak" and sucks out the body fluids. This is a wholly aquatic animal and, although it comes to the surface occasionally, it cannot fly.

Birds and Mammals of the Pond

Left: *The Cane Rat is a typical species of African swamps and rivers. It lives in the long grass and reeds, always near water. It is about fifty centimetres long and has rather bristly looking fur. For this reason it is sometimes called the Spiky Rat. It feeds on grasses and is particularly damaging to sugar-cane and maize. Like other riverside mammals it is an excellent swimmer.*

The Engineers of the Swamp

Only very few mammal species actually live in ponds. The mammals associated with ponds generally make their homes on dry land but spend a considerable time in the water in search of food. They frequently have thick fur, which retains the air, and webbed feet to help their swimming, as is the case with the beaver. Some of these mammals build deep dens on the shores with entrances below the water-line.

Underwater Fishing

The birds which live near ponds can be divided into four groups according to their feeding methods.

In the first group are the surface swimmers, such as ducks, which feed on anything they can reach by plunging their heads and the front part of their bodies in the water. The second group consists of diving birds, such as the Grebes which completely submerge themselves in order to catch their prey. The third group enters the water only briefly or skims along its surface as do the Marsh Terns. The last group includes waders, such as herons and sandpipers, which extract their food from the shallow waters or from the muddy edges with their long beaks.

Below: *The Harvest Mouse is a tiny rodent, some thirteen centimetres long, including its six-centimetre tail. The mouse uses its tail to help it climb, wrapping the tail around the slender stems to assist its progress. It runs swiftly and is an agile climber. It makes its nest by weaving grass into a ball shape suspended between stalks of grass. The Harvest Mouse feeds on grain and small insects. If these mice are too abundant they can become a pest in cornfields.*

Below: *The Water Shrew comes out at dusk at the edges of streams and ponds. It is an excellent swimmer and diver. It is found in Europe and Asia and feeds on insects and worms but will also attack small birds and fish. This shrew is about fifteen centimetres long, including the tail, and has thick, velvety fur which helps to keep the water out. It has many nocturnal enemies, owls and foxes being the main ones.*

Right: *Distinguished by their long necks and legs, the graceful herons and egrets are common water-birds in most parts of the world. There are many species and they are found in marshland, and flooded fields. Some even come insit urban developments as well as their more natural environment. They generally feed on fish, frogs or insects which they catch by spearing them with their long beaks. They often stalk their prey patiently beforehand. The two birds in the photograph are preening themselves, perched on a small clump of vegetation. The protruding stick on the right in the foreground gives the impression of an exceptionally long-legged bird: it is misleading; the birds' actual legs are hidden.*

Below: *The jabiru or Saddle-bill Stork is an African species found throughout central and southern Africa. It is not numerous and usually is seen solitary or in pairs in swampy districts. It stalks its prey in shallow water and eats frogs, fish, mammals and young birds, striking them with its strong bill. It nests in trees — as do the herons — making the nest out of sticks, and usually lays one white egg, rarely two.*

Pond Reptiles and Amphibians

Left: *The European Tree Frog,* Hyla arborea, *spends most of its life on trees and only enters the water during May and June to lay its eggs. The female lays up to one thousand eggs which are contained in a gelatinous substance about the size of a nut, which she attaches to an underwater plant. This animal is a native of north-west Africa, the Canary Islands, the Iberian peninsula, southern France and the north-west coast of Italy. It is dependent on water during the first stages of its development; later it can survive on dry land. Winter is spent in hibernation in a hole or beneath moss or under a stone.*

Below: *The Commom European Toad is a twilight and nocturnal animal and spends the daylight hours in winter and summer under stones and debris or in holes that it digs. It feeds on worms, insects and spiders and is itself the prey of large water-snakes. The male never grows bigger than ten centimetres but the female is usually larger. The eggs, varying in numbers between about two hundred and seven thousand are laid in a single gelatinous chain which the female winds around water-plants. The toad can live a long time and some have been known to survive for thirty-six years. They can exist without eating for periods of up to fifteen months. These toads are found in Europe and the temperate parts of Asia but they are absent from Ireland. They have a poison gland behind the eye which renders them distasteful to many predators. There are many species of toads throughout the temperate and tropical regions.*

Small Pond Animals

Amphibians are characteristic inhabitants of stagnant water. These cold-blooded animals are particularly abundant in both tropical and temperate regions. They live both on land and water, almost never in the sea where the salt would cause a continuous and fatal loss of water by osmosis through the skin. Amphibians lay their eggs in water where the young stages, breathing through gills, grow to the adult stage. The adults are perfectly adapted to life on land and breathe by means of lungs. They are therefore able to absorb oxygen from the air — through their lungs, and also from the water — through their skins. Some, such as newts, keep their tails in the adult stage and are in the order Urodela. Frogs, of which about 150 species are known in the world, lose their tails and are in the order Anura. Amphibians without legs belong to the order Apoda and there are about seventy species, all looking rather like large earthworms with elongated bodies. They live in burrows.

Reptiles have waterproof skins covered in scales and are mainly dry-land creatures; even in the early stages of their development they breathe through their lungs.

A number of the reptiles in the pond are predatory and, like other predators, they help to maintain a balance in their environment, preventing overpopulation by any one species.

Above: *The Red-eared Turtle or terrapin,* Pseumedys scripta, *is sought after as an aquarium turtle because it has a very brightly-coloured shell. It originates from parts of the United States of America, where it lives hidden in the muddy bottoms of rivers and ponds. In Spring the female lays from six to twenty-three eggs in holes dug in the sand a short distance from the water's edge. Adults can grow to a length of twenty-five centimetres.*

Below: *Alpine Newts are particularly abundant in central southern Europe. Their bodies have dark markings, except on the abdomen. During the mating-season, a smooth yellow and black crest develops on the male's back. They usually reach a size of eleven centimetres. Breeding occurs in Spring, except in high-altitude regions where this is delayed until summer. Several different species are present in Europe.*

Below: *Grass-snakes are variable in colour. When handled, they give off an evil-smelling secretion which helps to protect them. In spite of their popular name, they swim well, holding their heads above water. They lay up to twenty eggs, (sometimes more) and the young hatch in September. They feed on tadpoles, newts, frogs and other small animals. Grass-snakes are common throughout Europe.*

Below: *The Viperine Snake,* Natrix maura, *is found in sourthern Europe. It feeds on fish, under water, snapping them up as they swim past. In winter, it hibernates under boulders near the water. The eggs are laid in June and the young hatch in August. The Viperine Snake lives in ponds and marshes from sea-level up to 2,300 metres.*

Animals of the Seas and Inland Waters

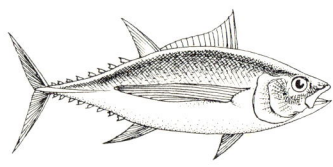

**Albacore or
Long-finned
Tunny**

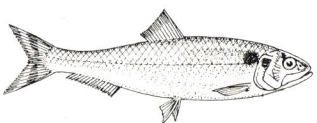

Allis Shad

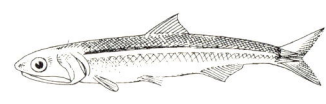

Anchovy

Albacore; Long-finned Tunny
(Thunnus = Germo alalunga)
The albacore is the smallest of the tunny fish, but unlike most tunny fish its flesh is whitish and not pink. These fish can be up to 100 centimetres in length and weigh up to 50 kilograms. They have very long sickle-shaped pectoral fins and a crescent-shaped, deeply forked tail fin. They live in shoals and occur mainly in warm and temperate seas.

Allis Shad *(Alosa (= Clupea) alosa = A. vulgaris)*
These fish belong to the herring family and are about 70 centimetres in length. Dorsally they are greyish-blue or have a greenish sheen, while the abdomen is silvery. Four species occur in the North Atlantic, the Mediterranean and the northern Pacific. They feed on minute aquatic animals, mainly pelagic crustaceans. In March they swim in huge shoals up rivers to their breeding-grounds, returning in the autumn with their young to the sea. In recent years they have disappeared from many rivers as a result of pollution and of measures to improve and control the flow of water.

Amphibians *(Amphibia)*
The word *amphibious* means living on land as well as in water. This group of animals is so-called, because in their larval stages they breathe through gills and live in water, but as adults they live mostly on land and breathe through lungs. They developed more than 350 million years ago and represent a' transitional form between fish and reptiles. They occur throughout the world with the exception of the polar regions. There are about 2,000 species sub-divided into three orders: frogs, newts and caecilians. The latter have a serpent-like body without limbs.

Anchovy *(Engraulis encrasicholus)*
Anchovies occur throughout the Mediterranean, the Black Sea, the Atlantic and the Baltic. They are small, about 16 centimetre in length, and are eaten by Man and by predators in the sea. The anchovy is itself a predator, feeding on fish, which are barely smaller than itself. In Spring and summer anchovies swim in great shoals in shallow water. They are of considerable economic importance and are sold fresh, salted or canned.

Angler fish: Fishing-frog; Monkfish *(Lophius piscatorious)*
Angler-fish belong to the group of fish that live on the bottom of the sea. They are up to 1.5 millimetres in length and weigh about 20 kilograms. They are among the largest of the monk-fish, having huge heads covered with small lobes and spiny rays. They have a wide mouth armed with many needle-like teeth. They mainly bury themselves in mud at depths of 200-300 millimetres. There they lie in wait for their prey, using the long free-standing ray on the dorsal fin, which has a lobe of skin at the tip, as a lure. They occur in the Mediterranean and the Atlantic.

Anura
In the adult stages anura are tailless amphibians. They have a squat body and a bare, slimy skin. They have a long tongue, which they can project forward at great speed to trap insects. Their hind-legs are longer and more powerful than the front ones and their toes are mostly webbed. Anura occur in all temperate and warm regions. They live near water, where the females generally lay their eggs. They feed on insects. To this group belong to the **Common Frog**, the **Tree Frog**, the **Toad** and the **Fire-Bellied Toad**.

Arapaima gigas
This is one of the world's largest known freshwater fish. They occur in the rivers of South America, principally in the Amazon. They can measure up to 4 millimetres in length. They have existed in their present form for over 300 million years. The water of the rivers in which they live has little oxygen and they can breathe air by means of a swim-bladder. They feed entirely on other fish and the *Arapaima* is one of the few fish which practise brood care. They are hunted with the harpoon. In Brazil, their flesh is cut into strips and eaten dried.

Argyropelecus hemigymnus
This is one of the species of fish which live at great depths in the Atlantic and mediterranean. It is silver-white in colour and has large telescopic eyes and luminescent organs along its body.

Barbel *(Barbus barbus)*
These fish belong to the carp family and have four long beard-threads on their protruding upper lip. They are about 50 centimetres long, sometimes longer, and weigh up to 8.5 kilograms. They are grey-green in colour and occur in the rivers of central and southern Europe, where they prefer fast-flowing water. Some species occur in western Asia. In the Spring they swim up-river in large shoals to their breeding-grounds, which are often high up in the mountains. They sometimes cover hundreds of kilometres when making this journey. As they put up a good fight when caught, they are popular with anglers. They are good to eat, but rather full of bones.

Bast Umber *(Sciaena cirrhosa)*
These fish belong to the family of *Sciaenidae* and occur in the Atlantic and the Mediterranean. They live near the coast over mud and sand and in river-mouths. They can be up to 70 centimetres in length and weigh 15 kilograms. Their scales are silver-grey with several wavy gold stripes running diagonally across the body. They feed principally on worms and snails. They are good to eat.

Blennies *(Blennioidei)*
Typical blennies, sometimes called Comb tooth Blennies, lack scales. They have a

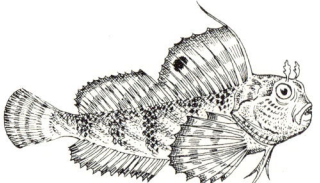

Blenny

slimy skin and a row of comb-like teeth in each jaw. They can vary in shape, being either long and eel-like, flatter and ribbon-like or cylindrical. They are not especially good to eat. Related species, such as the **Butterfly Blenny**, occur in the Meddditerranean.

Bony Fish *(Osteichthyes)*
This large sub-class includes almost all the familiar fish living in the sea or in fresh water. In contrast to the sharks and rays, which make up the cartilaginous group of fish, their skeleton is more or less strongly ossified. Their skin can be bare or covered with scales, but these again differ from those of the cartilaginous fish. Their gills are covered by bony flaps or opercula. There are about 20,000 different species.

Bullhead; Madtom; North American Catfish *(Ictalurus nebulosus)*
These fish came originally from the fresh waters of North America and were introduced into Europe at the turn of the century, where they soon became acclimatized and spread rapidly. Originally they were 45 centimetres in length but in Europe they are only 10-15 centimetres long. They have eight long barbels round the mouth. They live in standing or slow-flowing marshy water, stalking their prey among water-plants where they use their barbels as a lure. They feed on small fish and can cause great damage to other fish stocks.

Butterfly Fish *(Chaetodon auriga)*
This fish belongs to one of the largest of the coral fish families. It is one of the prettiest of all fish. They swim gracefully among the coral reefs in their many splendid colours and shapes, feeding on small crustaceans, polyps and worms. The *Auriga* has black stripes on a white background edged with red.

Cartilaginous Fish *(Chondrichthyes)*
This group of sea fish has a cartilaginous skeleton. Their gill-slits are not protected by bony gill-flaps. Their skin is covered with placoid scales, which are hard skin "teeth" projecting from the epidermis. Their mouth is underneath the head. They do not have an air-bladder and must therefore swim the whole time to avoid sinking to the bottom. To this group belong the sharks, rays, dogfish and skates. They are represented today by about 650 marine species.

Char *(Salvelinus alpinus)*
These fish belong to the family *Salmonidae* and are related to the trout. This species lives in alpine lakes and in the deep, cold seas round the British coasts. It migrates to the sea but returns to its original waters to breed. They are about 50 centimetres in length and vary in colouring usually matching their habitat. They are very good to eat.

Cod *(Gadus morhua)*
These fish are at home in shallower waters and along the continental shelf on both sides of the North Atlantic, mostly in depths of 40-250 millimetres. They can grow to 1.5 millimetres in length and weigh up to 45 kilograms. They feed on crustaceans, worms and molluscs. Normally they live in deeper water, returning to coastal waters in the Spring to breed or to feed. They are caught in large numbers at this time. Their delicate white flesh is eaten in a variety of ways, and it can be salted or smoked. In addition to its use as a source of food, it is used medicinally as the source of cod-liver oil and as animal feed and fertilizer.

Coelenterates *(Coelenterata)*
This group of animals, characterized by their single body cavity, is divided into three classes, the Hydrozoa, the Scyphozoa and the Anthozoa. Almost all live in the sea either singly or in colonies. Their tube-like body is made up of two layers: the ectoderm, or outer layer; and the endoderm, or inner layer. The latter covers the inner gut cavity. The single body cavity serves as stomach and gut and has only one opening. There are two distinct forms: (1) the polyps, which are sedentary, attached at their base to any surface and with their mouth opening uppermost; (2) the free-swimming medusae, to which the jelly-fish belong. The latter look like an umbrella and have their mouth opening hanging downwards. Corals and sea-anemones belong to the former group of fixed polyps.

Common Carp *(Cyprinus carpio)*
Carp was a favourite dish in the times of the Greeks and Romans; it is still regarded as a great delicacy. Nowadays they are artificially bred in special ponds almost world-wide and in the rice-fields of Italy. They are generally 50-60 centimetres in length and weigh 2-3 kilograms. They occur naturally in rivers and fresh water throughout the world, provided that the water is not too cold. They prefer calm water with a muddy bottom and plenty of vegetation. They are blackish-grey or brownish in colour, although those which live in rivers are lighter than those living in muddy ponds.

Common Mackerel *(Scomber scomber)*
These fish are the chief representatives of the mackerel family, the *Scombridae*, and are found in large numbers in the Atlantic, the North Sea, the Baltic and the Mediterranean. They are up to 50 centimetres in length and bluish-green in colour with numerous diagonal stripes. Mackerel swim in great shoals just below the surface of the sea. They have no air-bladder and can therefore dive very swiftly into deep water when escaping from predators and similarly rise quickly to the surface. Mackerel fishing is of considerable commercial importance as mackerel are very good to eat, – fresh, smoked or canned.

Common Mussel *(Mytilus edulis)*
This edible mussel occurs widely in the Atlantic and the Mediterranean and is much in demand for the table. They are 5-10 centimetres long and have brownish-black oval shells. They are found in large numbers adhering to rocks and piles by means of an especially strong tuft of fine silky threads called a byssus. The cultivation of these mussels is an important industry in France, Holland and Italy.

Common Toad *(Bufo bufo)*
The Common Toad is found throughout almost the whole of Europe and in large areas of Asia. A subspecies occurs in North Africa. The females are about 15 centimetres in length. Their skin varies in colour and is covered with warts and lobes. Toads spend the day hidden, emerging at night to hunt insects and worms. They mate in ponds, water-filled ditches or larger stretches of water. Their eggs are attached together in long strings which become wound round plants in the water.

Common Tunny *(Thunnus thynnus)*
These fish have been known since ancient times and are sometimes grouped with the mackerel. They are up to 3 millimetres in length. Their slender body is dorsally blue and ventrally and laterally white. Tunny are fast swimmers and feed on sardines and anchovies. They live in deep

**Bullhead or
North American Catfish**

Butterfly Fish

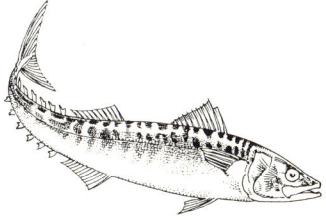

Common Mackerel

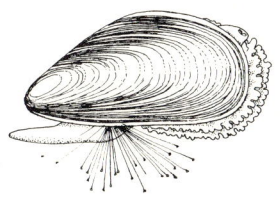

Common Mussel

Red Coral

Corvina nigra

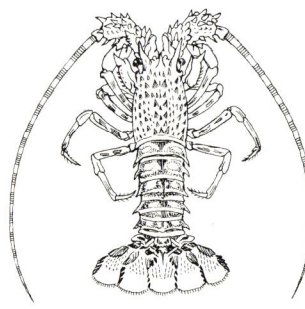

Crayfish

Dentex

water in the Atlantic and the Mediterranean. At breeding-time they approach the coasts of North Africa, eastern Sicily and Sardinia in huge shoals, and are caught in large numbers. Their firm pink flesh is economically very important for the countries around the Mediterranean.

Corals

Corals and sea-anemones (Anthozoa) are a class belonging to the coelenterates. **Red Coral** or **Precious Coral** occurs in the Mediterranean chiefly along the coast of North Africa, around Sardinia and in the Bay of Naples. It lives in depths of 80-200 metres and forms tree-like branched colonies on rocks. It can be any colour from pure white to deep red. The skeleton is of calcareous sclerites or made of a horny substance and surrounded by a softer casing, in which the polyps are embedded. Coral is much in demand for jewellery.

Corvina nigra

These fish with their dark bronze, shimmering scales and black-edged fins owe their name to the crow-like noise which they make. They live in small shoals over rocky ground in shallow water. They can be up to 70 centimetres in length and feed on crustaceans and algae.

Crayfish; Spiny Lobster *(Palinurus vulgaris)*

These are crustaceans which occur in the Mediterranean and the Atlantic, principally along the French and Spanish coasts. They can be 50 centimetres long and have long antennae (which they use to ward off enemies or other crayfish). Their tail is fan-shaped. They do not have pincers. Their carapace is brownish-violet in colour and turns red when boiled. They live on rocky ground at depths of 15-100 metres in coastal waters. Because of their excellent meat, they are caught in large numbers, usually in pots.

Crustaceans *(Crustacea)*

Crustaceans are principally aquatic arthropods which have an external skeleton, in many cases encrusted with calcified layers. They vary in size from only 1 millimetre to the 3 metres of tropical species. Their body is divided into head, thorax and abdomen. On each segment there are paired appendages which serve as jaws, legs, feelers or to catch food. As a rule the head has two pairs of feelers or antennae and three pairs of feeding appendages. Most crustaceans moult periodically as their body grows. To the *Crustacea* belong not only the well-known crabs, prawns, lobsters and shrimps but also the Isopoda, sand-hoppers and barnacles.

Date Mussel *(Lithophaga lithophaga)*

Date Mussels are molluscs and owe their name to their brown colour and the shape of their shells. They are about 10 centimetres in length. With the aid of an acid secreted from a gland in the mantle, they bore round holes in stones and rocks, in which they live. They occur in the Mediterranean and are very good to eat.

Dentex; Toothed Sparus *(Dentex dentex)*

These fish belong to the family of the Sparidae and are popular with both amateur and professional fishermen. They can grow to over 1 metre in length and weigh up to 10 kilograms. They feed on sea-grass in the Mediterranean and in the eastern Atlantic. At breeding-time they are found along coasts. They are unmistakable in appearance. Their body is laterally very compressed and they have a high concave forehead line and a wide mouth with powerful catching teeth. They have only one

dorsal fin, the front part of which has long hard rays. Dorsally they are bluish-green and laterally they are silver-pink with dark blue spots.

Echinoderms; Spiny-skinned Animals *(Echinodermata)*

These spiny-skinned marine animals belong to an ancient phylum of invertebrates. They all have characteristic shapes. The phylum includes all starfish, sea-urchins, sea-lilies, sea-cucumbers and brittlestars. Echinoderms have a calcareous skeleton of movable plates set in the body-wall, on which there are usually spines or nodules. A particular feature of echinoderms is their small suckers or tube-feet, which are present in most species. These are connected to a water vascular system which alternately fills and empties, contracting and relaxing the "feet". In this way, the animal can move slowly forward. All echinoderms live on the bottom and some, like the sea-lilies, are sedentary. Sea-urchins and starfish move by means of their tube-feet and can cover 5 centimetres in one minute.

Edible Frog *(Rana esculenta)*

The Edible Frog is found throughout Europe. They are up to 7.5 centimetres in length, although the female can be longer. Their back is mostly green and often has black spots. Their skin is either smooth or warty. They live in ponds or standing water, marshes or ditches. They remain all their life in one place. They feed on worms, snails and insects. At mating-time the males make their familiar croaking call, using the two large vocal-sacs at the sides of the mouth. The females lay their eggs in water in clumps, each clump containing up to 10,000 eggs. The larvae hatch after eight days. Their development into the adult frog lasts four months.

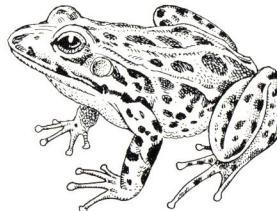

Edible Frog

Eels
A Common Freshwater Eel
(Anguilla anguilla)

All eels have a snake-like, elongated, cylindrical body, whether they occur in the sea or in fresh water. The females of the common freshwater eel are from 90-100 centimetres in length and they weigh 5-7 kilograms. The males are appreciably smaller. Their skin is thick and slimy and covered with minute scales, which are barely visible. The common eel is found in fresh water and brackish water in Europe, North America and North Africa. After six or ten years they return to the sea, finding their way instinctively and covering distances of 5,000-7,000 kilometres without feeding, to reach their breeding-grounds in the Sargasso Sea in the Atlantic. There they lay their eggs, at a depth of 500 metres, and die. The newly-emerged larva are transparent and shaped like a willow leaf. They immediately start on the return journey and, amazingly, find their way to the river, from which their parents set out. The Freshwater Eel is edible and regarded as a delicacy.

Conger Eel *(Conger conger)*

In contrast to the Freshwater Eel, the Conger Eel can be up to 3 metres long and weigh 65 kilograms. They feed on other fish and occur in almost all seas, preferring rocky coasts; they are also found in brackish water in river estuaries. During the day they hide in cracks and fissures, spending the night hunting molluscs, crustaceans and fish. Very little is known of their breeding habits. Their flesh has a delicate flavour and they are particularly good to eat.

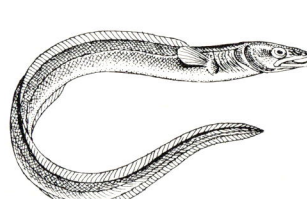

Conger Eel

Moray Eel *(Muraena helena)*

This eel occurs over rocky ground in the Mediterranean, the southern Atlantic and the Indian Ocean. They are about 150

Moray Eel

centimetres long and have a wide mouth with pointed teeth. Their skin is bare, having no scales, and it is slimy. They are brownish in colour with white or yellow spots. They feed on crustaceans, fish and molluscs. They often bite and, as they produce a toxic slime in the mouth cavity, this bite can be dangerous to Man. They are edible and regarded as a delicacy.

Electric Ray (Torpedo marmorata)
The most important characteristics of this ray are the two electric organs between the pectoral fins and the head. These organs consist of many hexagonal prisms, each one of which consists of up to 10-12 overlapping plates. They are like the elements of a battery. Electric Rays occur in temperate waters in the Atlantic and the Mediterranean. They use their electric organs both as a means of defence and to stun their prey. Their attack is harmless to Man but the relatively powerful discharge (up to 220 volts) can cause temporary paralysis. They are not good to eat.

Flying Gurnard
(Dactylopterus volitans)
These fish are about 40 centimetres in length and occur exclusively in temperate seas. They are bizarre-looking fish and their pectoral fins are divided into two parts. The front part is seperate and very small and is used by the fish as a feeler or means of locomotion along the bottom of the sea. It is not certain, but it is commonly believed, that it can make short flying leaps over the surface of the water, using the very large rear part of the pectoral fin. These fish vary in colour from bright red, silver, blue, brown to reddish brown and they are mottled with spots and stripes.

Garfish; Greenbone (Belone belone)
These are large fish, which occur in all European waters. They are 70-100 centimetres in length and have an elongated arrow-shaped body with long, pointed jaws and small pointed teeth. They are dorsally blue-green and their bones are green, which accounts for their name. They are predators. They approach the coast to breed and will enter lagoons. They are very popular with anglers and are particularly good to eat.

Gilt-head (Sparus auratus)
These fish live along the rocky coasts of the eastern Atlantic and the Mediterranean. They are covered with shimmering golden-yellow scales and have one long gold spot at the end of the gill-flaps. They are good to eat, having firm, tasty flesh. They feed principally on molluscs and crustaceans, which they can easily crack open with their powerful teeth (they have 3-5 rows). Their favourite hunting-grounds are cultivated mussel-beds, where they cause great damage. They are caught chiefly in the summer and autumn.

Gobies (Gobiidae)
This is a large family of fish living in the littoral zones of tropical and temperate seas. In some species the pelvic fins are set well forward and have grown together to form a sucker disc, with which the fish can attach themselves to stones and rocks. Gobies are quite small, the smallest measuring only 11 millimetres. **Eleotris fusca,** one of the **Sleeper Gobies,** is very common in the Indian and Pacific Oceans. They are found from the coast of East Africa to Polynesia. They live chiefly in brackish water and in mangrove swamps, hidden under stones and empty shells. Another species, *Butis butis*, has a large flat head and a large mouth. They also occur in brackish water from East Africa to Australia. They are mainly reddish-brown in colour with red spots and their fins have a yellow border.

Goldfish (Cyprinidae)
This well-known member of the carp family can be up to 25 centimetres in length and comes from China. Many varieties have been developed. In their natural environment they are covered with greenish scales and have insignificant fins. Red specimens which occasionally occur were bred and imported into Europe as ornamental fish. Since then they have been bred in special aquariums. Glowing colours, some with spots or stripes, have been developed. One of these varieties is the **Veiltail Goldfish** which has enlarged tail fins. Another variation is the **Lion-head Goldfish.**

Greater Weever (Trachinus draco)
These fish, which are 35-45 centimetres long, live over sand in the shallow waters of the Mediterranean and the eastern Atlantic. They bury themselves in the sand, waiting for small crustaceans, fish and other prey. Their poisonous spines are much feared by bathers and fishermen and they can cause painful wounds. These spines are situated on the gill-covers and along the dorsal fin.

Great Pipe-fish (Syngnathus acus)
These fish are related to the sea-horses. Their body is long and thin and their mouth is tube-like and without teeth. They can be up to 40 centimetres long and occur in European coastal waters from Biscay to northern Norway, over snd and rocks. They feed on fish-spawn, small crustaceans and worms. The males have a brood-pocket in which the females lay their eggs. The eggs remain there until the young hatch after five weeks.

Hake (Merluccius merluccius)
This member of the cod family occurs in the eastern Atlantic, the Baltic and the Mediterranean in shallow or deep water. They are 50-80 centimetres in length. Dorsally they are grey-brown to black, laterally lighter and ventrally silver. They have a brown lateral stripe. Their body is quite slim. They are predators, hunting mainly herring, mackerel and sardines. At breeding-time they approach the coasts and are then caught in large numbers, since they are particularly good to eat.

Hermit Crabs; False Crabs
(Paguridae) (Crustacea)
There are several species of the decapoda, which, unlike other crabs, have a soft-skinned, unprotected abdomen, with which they adhere inside empty shells. These shells are often then covered with sea-anemones, thereby forming one of the best known examples of symbiosis in the animal kingdom. Symbiosis is the association of two different organisms, which live attached to each other, or one as a tenant of the other, and which contribute to each other's support: the hermit crab is protected from its enemies by the sea-anemone and in return the sea-anemone is transported by the crab, enabling it to feed more easily.

Herring (Clupea harengus)
Herrings are probably Man's most important source of food from the sea. Enormous quantities of them are eaten either fresh, salted or smoked. They measure from 15-40 centimetres and are dorsally blue-green but laterally silver. They live at about 200 metres depth and will swim great distances in fantastically large shoals in search of food and breeding-grounds. They breed on sandy, shallow, sea-banks and occur in the northern Atlantic and in the sea of northern Europe.

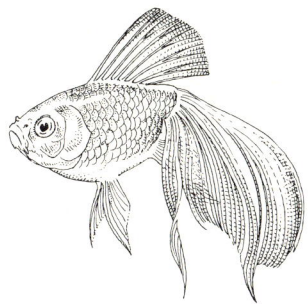

Goldfish

Greater Weever

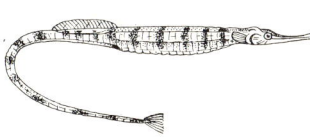

Great Pipe-fish

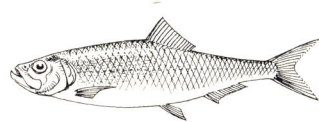

Herring

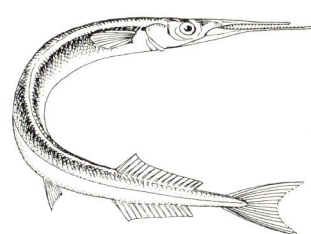

Garfish or Greenbone

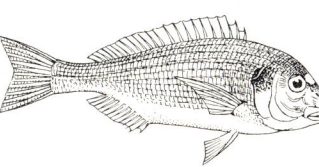

Gilt-head

Sleeper Goby

The North Sea Herring is specific to the North Sea.

John Dory (Zeus faber)

These fish have a laterally compressed body and a large head with wide mouth. They measure about 1 metre. Their scales are either golden or grey-green to match their surroundings. Behind the pectoral fin on both sides they have a large white-edged dark spot. They generally occur in deeper water, from 100-200 metres, in the Atlantic and the Mediterranean. They are found following shoals of young herring, on which they feed. In German it is known as Peter's Fish and is said to be named after the Apostle, who found a coin (with which to pay his tribute) in the mouth of this fish. The two spots are said to mark the impression of the saint's fingers. In English, the word Dory is presumably derived from The French *dore*, which means "golden" or "gilded".

Lampreys (Petromyzonidae)

These fish-like animals belong to the class of *Cyclostomata* and have an eel-like body, a nodulose skeleton and a slimy skin without scales. They only have a very small single nose opening. Their German common name of *Neunaugen* or "Nine-eyes" arose from a misunderstanding on the part of earlier observers, who interpreted the nostil, as well as the seven round gill-slits, as eyes. The mouth is a round sucker armed with horny teeth. Lampreys attach themselves by means of this oral sucker to the body of their prey, gradually eating their way into the flesh of the living fish to suck out blood. They are a great delicacy. The **Sea Lamprey** (Petromyzon marinus) occurs in the Mediterranean and in the Atlantic and is 60-90 centimetres in length. This species generally lives in quite deep water but in Spring and summer it returns to the rivers to breed. All lampreys are good to eat. Related species are the **River Lamprey** (Lampetra fluviatilis) and the **Brook Lamprey** (Lampetra planeri)

Lamprey

Latimeria chalumnae

On 22 December, 1938 a fish from the order *Crossopterygii* was caught off the coast of South Africa near the town of East London. Until this date this order had only been known from fossils and it was assumed that these fish had died out over 70 million years ago. This "living fossil" was named *Latimeria* after the director of the Natural History Museum of East London, Dr. Latimer. The fish measured 1.5 metres and weighted 58 kilograms and was steely-blue in colour. Its head and body were covered with round scales as well as warts and spines. Subsequently, further specimens were caught off the coast of Madagascar and around the Comoro Islands

Latimeria chalumnae

Lesser Devil-fish (Mobula mobular)

These are enormous rays, whose diamond-shaped body can measure up to 5 metres across. They live in the Atlantic but can occur in the western Mediterranean. Their flesh is tough and does not taste good. They owe their name to the two horns on their head, which look like devil's horns. Inspite of their weight, they can leap high out of the water, landing back with a loud splash. There is an even larger ray, *Manta birostris,* which can be up to 7 metres across and weigh 2 tonnes.

Lung-fish (Dipnoi)

Lung-fish existed in large numbers many years ago, but today there are only a few species left and these are threatened with extinction. They are like "living fossils". Their elongated eel-like body is covered with scales and their head is broad. Their skeleton is, to a large extent, cartilaginous. They have lungs as well as gills and can

breathe air. They can survive long periods of drought by burying themselves in the mud. The best known species are: **Australian Lung-fish** (Neoceratodus forsteri), which occurs today only in a few rivers in Queensland, Australia. They are the most primitive in form and are plump and covered with large cycloid scales. **Ethiopian Lung-fish** (Protopterus aethiopicus), which are 80-90 centimetres in length and live in the inland waters of East Africa. **South American Lung-fish** (Lepidosiren paradoxa), which are shaped like eels and are about 1 metre in length with long, fan-shaped fins. They occur exclusively in South America.

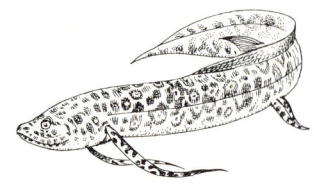

Ethiopian Lung-fish

Madrepore Corals (Madreporaria)

These are coelenterates which occur in tropical and sub-tropical seas, usually forming fixed colonies. They only thrive in temperate, clear, oxygen-rich water. These corals build tree-like colonies, in which countless individual polyps live as a thin film on the calcareous skeleton, which is continuously deposited beneath each polyp. These colonies are very elaborate and varied in shape. Large conglomerations of them form into reefs or atolls and they can be very extensive. The largest coral reef is the Great Barrier Reef, which is about 2,000 kilometres long and extends along the north-east coast of Australia.

Molluscs (Mollusca)

This is a phylum of invertebrates, whose numerous species almost all live in the sea. They have a soft body without a skeleton and in most species the body is protected by a shell. Although they may vary in appearance, size and habits, they all have the same sack-like body, with a ventral foot (a muscular organ used for locomotion) and a mantle, which is a fold of skin projecting from the top or back. The mantle secretes a calcareous substance, which forms the shell or housing. Between the mantle and the foot there is usually a mantle cavity, which contains the respiratory organs. Among the many molluscs are the snails (Gastropoda), the bivalves (Bivalvia), such as clams and mussels, and the cephalopods (Cephalopoda) such as cuttlefish, octopus and squid.

Mullet (Mugilidae)

All species belonging to this family have a slender, fleshy body, which is usually over 60 centimetres in length and weighs over 6 kilograms. The mouth of the mullet bends upwards and the upper jaw is broken by a mouth slit, into which the protruding lower jaw fits. The first of the two dorsal fins has only four rays. They live over mud and feed on smaller animal or plant organisms. Their flesh is firm and very tasty. There are more than 100 species.

Mugil cephalus can be up to 90 centimetres in length and occurs in all warmer seas and in the Mediterranean. They are dorsally ash-grey and ventrally white. They have 9-10 lighter longitudinal stripes on their sides. They are also very good to eat.

Mullet (Mullidae)

There are 42 species of this family living in the coastal waters of warm and temperate seas. The following species live in the Mediterranean:

Striped Mullet (Mullus surmuletus), which grows to a length of 40 centimetres and has a large head and a steep forehead line. Two long barbels hang down from the mouth. Its scales are red and laterally it has yellow longitudinal stripes. It lives over rocky ground in fairly shallow water.

Red Mullet (Mullus barbatus), which is somewhat smaller than the Striped Mullet, living mainly over sand and mud at depths of up to 200 metres. These mullet are particularly good to eat.

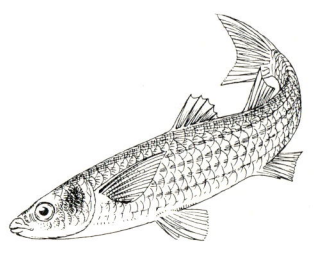

Mullet

Oyster

Pearl fish and Sea-cucumber

Pelamid or Belted Bonito

Perch

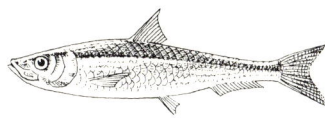

Pilchard

Oar-fish (Regalecus glesne)

These are ribbon-like, almost transparent fish, which can measure up to 9 metres in length and which live in the deep water of all oceans. Their scales are silvery with a bluish sheen and dark spots. Their fins extend over the whole length of the back and are gleaming red. They are rarely caught and little is therefore known about them.

Oyster; Flat Oyster (Ostrea edulis)

These molluscs attach themselves at a very early age, by means of thin threads, to rocks and stony ground in depths of up to 50 metres and there they stay. They are found along all European coasts from Norway to the Black Sea. Their shells are unequal, very rough and greenish-grey in colour. Oysters are cultivated in artificial beds in France, Spain, England and Italy, as they are a highly prized delicacy.

Pearl Fish (Carapus acus)

These curious fish are 10-20 centimetres in length and belong to the sub-order of *Ophidioidei*. They are a good example of commensalism in the animal kingdom – the sharing of food and living-quarters. These fish live in the gut of the sea-cucumber, which they only leave at night when searching for food. As soon as it has satisfied its hunger with small crustaceans and larvae, the fish returns to its hiding-place, penetrating with its tail into the anus of the sea-cucumber. It then wriggles its thin, scale-less body up into the gut of its host, leaving only its head outside.

Pelamid; Belted Bonito (Sarda mediterranea)

These fish belong to the mackerel family and are fished along the coasts of Portugal, in the eastern Mediterranean and in the Black Sea. They are 30-80 centimetres in length and similar to tunny. They are in fact often sold as tunny. They are bluish in colour with black stripes.

Perch (Perca fluviatilis)

These fish occur in inland waters in central and northern Europe, northern Asia and in North America. They are very good to eat and, as a result, popular with anglers. They vary in length from 20-45 centimetres. Dorsally their scales are greenish with 6-7 dark diagonal stripes on their sides. Laterally they are lighter and their abdomen is greyish-white. In winter perch live in deep water but in Spring they swim in shoals into shallower water along the banks, where the females lay their eggs in a broad network of ribbons, which become attached to stones and plants. The young fish hatch after fourteen days and remain together in shoals.

Pike (Esox lucius)

Pike occur throughout Europe, Asia and North America in fresh water. The females can be up to 150 centimetres in length, while the males are only 1 metre long. They have a long head with a flat snout shaped like a duck-bill, and pointed teeth. They feed mainly on fish, including their own species. As a result, they are not popular with fish breeders. A single pike in one fish-pond can cause great damage to stocks. Large pike will even prey on small waterfowl and small mammals.

Pilchard (Sardina pilchardus)

This representative of the herring family is of great economic importance and is eaten either fresh or preserved in salt or oil. It occurs in shoals in the Mediterranean and Atlantic and measures 12-18 centimetres. These fish live in quite deep water but swim into coastal water in the Spring to breed.

Piranha; Piraya (Serrasalmus piraya)

These fish live in the waters of the Amazon and the Orinoco and are greatly feared. Their body is about 30 centimetres long, very high and laterally compressed. They are strongly-coloured. Their blunt mouth is full of extraordinarily powerful and sharp teeth. They swim mostly in shoals and feed mainly on fish. They are invariably attracted by fresh blood and they will attack large mammals (including Man), if these fall wounded into the water. They gnaw their prey and in a very short time only the bare bones are left.

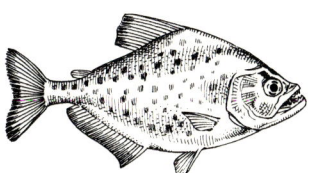

Piranha or Piraya

Plaice (Pleuronectes platessa)

These are flatfish which resemble the sole in taste and appearance. They occur along the Atlantic coasts in Europe and in the eastern Mediterranean. They are usually about 50 centimetres long and have a flat body. Only the upper surface of the body is pigmented and it is grey with red dots. Both eyes are on one side. They live over sand and feed on worms and mussels. They grow very slowly and can live up to fifty years.

Plankton

Plankton is composed of a multitude of minute organisms, which float freely in the water, drifting with the currents, waves or tides. **Phytoplankton** is the name given to the floating plants which are mainly single-celled algae, fungi and bacteria. **Zooplankton** refers to the animals of the plankton. The latter include the larvae of sea-urchins, starfish and shrimps, and fish spawn. Plankton is the major source of food for countless aquatic animals.

Porcupine Fish (Diodon hystrix)

These fish live among coral reefs in tropical seas. They are up to 70 centimetres in length and their oval body is covered with 2-5 centimetre long spines. When faced with danger they can puff up their body by filling their stomach with water, until they are like a spine-covered ball or a rolled-up hedgehog. When puffed up, they turn somersaults while swimming, just like a ball. When the danger is over, they expel the water.

Porcupine Fish

Protozoans (Protozoa)

These are microscopically small, single-celled animals, which have their own sub-kingdom in the animal world. They represent the simplest and most primitive form of animal-life and will be found, wherever there is water. Many live in or on other organisms, or as parasites in plants or animals. Most of them have a permanent recognizable structure and shape. There are, however, protozoans, such as the *Amoeba*, which do not have a constant shape. Countless numbers of protozoans live in the plankton.

Pufferfish; Puffers (Tetraodontidae)

The scientific name of these fish, which occur in very many shapes, means "with four teeth", for they have two powerful teeth on each of the lower and upper jaw, which form a sort of beak. They live along the coasts or coral reefs in tropical seas and vary in length from 6-90 centimetres and weigh from a few grammes to 6.5 kilograms. When attacked or alarmed, they can inflate their body with air or water into a huge ball. The skin of some species is used in Japan to make lanterns and lampshades.

Pumpkinseed Sunfish (Lepomis gibbosus)

Sunfish, a family of freshwater fish, were only introduced into Europe from North America at the end of the last century. Today they are widely distributed in ponds and standing water. A few species are

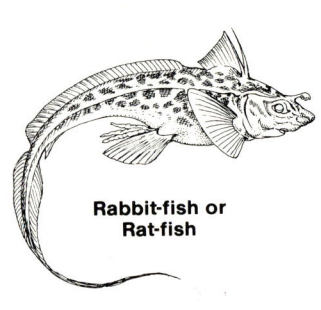

Rabbit-fish or Rat-fish

Rainbow Wrasse

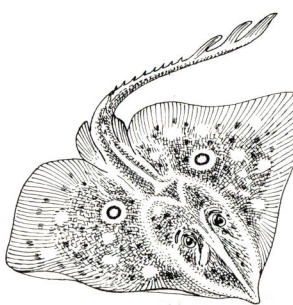

Thornback Ray

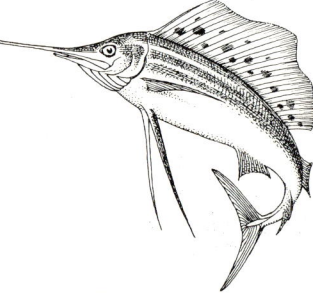

Sailfish

Salmon

popular in aquariums. The Pumpkinseed Sunfish measures about 10 centimetres and its scales are attractively coloured: bronze with blue and red mottling. Sunfish practise brood-care and build carefully prepared hollows, in which they lay their eggs.

Rabbit-fish; Rat-fish (Chimaera monstrosa)

Chimaeras or rat-fish are cartilaginous fish related to the dogfish and sharks. The rabbit-fish is found throughout the eastern Atlantic and in the Mediterranean. They are up to 1 metre in length and live at depths of up to 1,000 metres. They feed mainly on crustaceans and molluscs. Their red-brown body has silver-blue mottling and is broader at the front, the head is compressed and the long tail is string-like. The males have a knobby clasping organ in the middle of the forehead. They are not good to eat.

Rainbow Wrasse (Coris julis)

This is a particularly beautiful member of the wrasse family of *Labridae*, which occur in the Mediterranean and in the Atlantic. Several hundred species belong to this family and occur mostly in warmer seas. They are relatively small predators, feeding on all sorts of animals living on the sea-bottom. Their family name is derived from their particularly thick lips. A characterisitic of the wrasse is to bury itself in the sand to sleep, or to lean on a rock. More colourful still is the **Peacock Wrasse** (Crenilabrus pavo), which only occurs in the warmer waters of the Mediterranean and which measures up to 30 centimetres. It is bright green with red and blue spots. These colourful fish are especially popular in seawater aquariums.

Rays (Rajidae)

These are cartilaginous fish, found in numerous forms in temperate and cold seas. They have greatly enlarged pectoral fins, so that their body is diamond-shaped. Their tail is long and thin and their skin is rough and covered with spines. Their mouth and gills are on the ventral side and their eyes on the back. Rays live on the bottom of the sea and feed principally on fish, crustaceans and molluscs. A well-known species which occurs in the Channel and in the Atlantic is the **Thornback Ray** (Raja clavata) This fish can be 120 centimetres in length and it has powerful spines on its tail and back.

Sailfish (Istiophorus albinans)

The name of these fish is derived from their enormously enlarged dorsal fin. They can be more than 3 metres in length and weigh up to 55 kilograms. They occur in warm zones in the Atlantic. Their upper jaw is elongated and spear-shaped but not as strong as that of the sword-fish. They use it as a weapon, attacking large shoals of fish.

Salmon (Salmo salar)

Salmon have been of considerable economic importance since ancient times, as their flesh is delicious – fresh, smoked or salted. These fish are usually about 1 metre in length. Dorsally their scales are blue-grey, but laterally they are silver. They have a single dark grey adipose fin. When one or two years old the young salmon come down to the cold waters of the Atlantic, having spent their youth in the upper reaches of rivers. When three or four they return to the rivers, from which they came. They swim hundreds of kilometres up-river, leaping up waterfalls or over rapids. They breed and lay their eggs in the clear waters of mountain streams.

Sapphirine Gurnard (Trigla hirundo)

These fish live in the Mediterranean and

the Atlantic, over sand or rocks in shallow or quite deep water. They are 50-60 centimetres in length and are reddish but lighter ventrally. Their fins are edged with blue. Their head is protected with overlapping, reinforced scales and their snout is lengthened forwards. They have three rays in front of the pectoral fins, which are used as feelers and locomotion organs. A rare species is *Trigloporus africanus* which lives in much deeper water. Using the bladder and a special muscle, these fish are able to produce a peculiar growling noise.

Sawfish (Pristis pectinatus)

These fish, which are related to the rays, have a flat, elongated snout, which has lateral, stout, tooth-like structures on each side resembling a saw. This snout can measure up to 2 metres and the whole fish can be up to 6 metres long. The flattened body has sail-like, enlarged pectoral fins. The skin is grey and covered with fine granules. They live in warm seas near the shore and often swim into large tropical rivers. Using their saw, they burrow in the bottom searching for mussels and snails or attack shoals of fish. They are caught not only for their flesh, but also for their skin, from which excellent leather is produced. Their fins are regarded as a great delicacy in China.

Sea Bass (Roccus = Morone labrax)

These fish belong to the sub-order *Percoidei* and are caught in the Bay of Biscay, off the coast of Portugal and in the Mediterranean, using a line or a basket. They are most common in the eastern Atlantic. They are greedy predators and are found in groups even in fairly deep water near coasts or in mouths of rivers. They are silver-grey and can measure up to 80 centimetres and weight 5-7 kilograms.

Sea Bream (Oblada melanura)

These fish belong to the large family of Sea Bream and occur along the coasts of the Atlantic and in the Mediterranean. They are 15-30 centimetres in length and have a large black spot ringed with white in front of the tail. They are not predatory, belonging to the group of bream that feed on plants. They are very good to eat.

Sea-horse (Hippocampus)

There are several species of the sea-horse and they are related to the pipe-fish. They are unique in appearance. Their snout is elongated into a trunk and their long tail has no fin. Their head is at right-angles to their body and they swim in an upright position. Their body is covered with bony plates. They are about 15 centimetres long and live among algae, where they are well camouflaged, being brownish, reddish or greenish in colour and either striped or spotted. The males have a brood pocket on the abdomen, in which the females lay their eggs. The eggs remain in the pocket until the larvae hatch.

Sea-urchins (Echinoidea)

Sea-urchins belong to the class of echinoderms and have a spherical, egg-shaped or heart-shaped body, about 5-18 centimetres across. Their skeleton is shell-like and completely covered with long spines. The lower spines are used as stilts in locomotion. The anal opening is on the top of the body; the mouth opening is on the opposite side. The mouth has a complicated chewing apparatus, consisting of five powerful teeth and known as Aristotle's lantern. Most sea-urchins are omnivorous.

Serrranidae

There are 500 large and powerful species in this family of fish and they are all good to eat. They almost all live in the sea. They

Sapphirine Gurnard

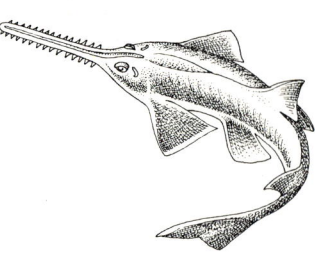

Sawfish

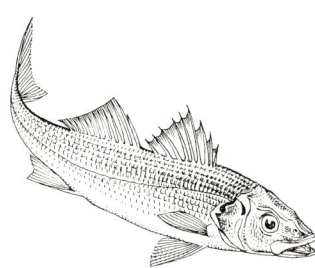

Sea Bass

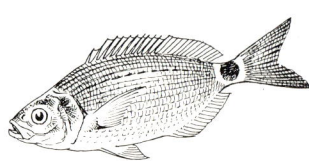

Sea Bream

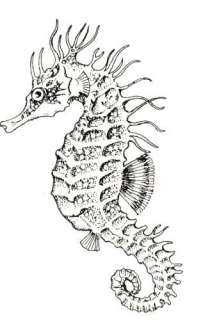

Sea-horse

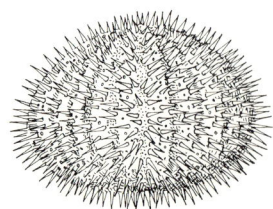

Sea-urchin

are popular sport fish for divers but are difficult to catch. They are voracious predators with well-equipped jaws and very wide mouths. Their fins have strong spines. A small representative of the family, the **Sea Perch** or **Learned Rock-fish** *(Serranellus scriba)*, lives among the rocks and clefts on the Mediterranean coast. It is only about 30 centimetres in length and has one dorsal fin, which is serrated. It is mainly reddish-yellow and has seven broad, blackish-blue diagonal bands, which run along its entire body. Ventrally, and on the lower jaw, it is yellow. All its fins have a reddish-blue edge.

Sharks; Dogfish *(Selachoidei)*

Sharks belong to the group of cartilaginous fish, of which there are numerous families and about 250 different species. The following are among the best known.

Great Blue Shark *(Carcharhinus)*

These sharks occur in all warm and temperate seas and in the Mediterranean, but only rarely in the North Sea. They can be up to 6 metres in length. They are armed with terrible teeth and are voracious predators, always attracted by the smell of blood, snapping at anything swimming in the water, including Man. They are not popular with fishermen, as they will plunder their filled nets.

Spurdog; Picked Dogfish
(Acanthias (= Squallus) acanthias)

These are smaller sharks, measuring only a little over 1 metre. They are most common in the northern Atlantic. They have long, powerful spines or spurs (in front of each of the two dorsal fins) which they use as weapons and which account for their name. When young, they are irregularly spotted but later they become greyish-brown and ventrally yellow. They swim close to the shore in small shoals and feed mainly on fish. They are not dangerous to Man. They are caught for their flesh and their oil.

Smooth Hound

These sharks belong to the family of *Triakidae* and are found in the Mediterranean. *Mustelus mustelus*, which is about 70 centimetres in length occurs in the south and *Mustelus asterias*, which is up to 2 metres long, in the north. They are quite harmless. They prefer areas where the bottom is sandy, and they feed mainly on worms, molluscs and crustaceans. *Mustelus asterias* has white spots on its greyish-brown back. They are viviparous, giving birth to live young.

Hammerhead Shark *(Sphyrna zygaena)*

These sharks occur in tropical and subtropical seas. Their head is characteristically hammer- or T-shaped. They can be up to 4 metres in length. Their teeth are particularly sharp, triangular and serrated. They live over muddy ground in depths up to 400 metres, feeding on molluscs, crustaceans and rays. They can be dangerous to Man. Their skin is bluish-grey and slightly granular. It is widely processed for leather. They are viviparous.

Grey-Shark; Six-Gilled Shark *(Hexanchus griseus)*

These sharks can be up to 5 metres long and feed principally on fish. They belong to the group of sharks which have comb-like, jagged teeth.

Scyliorhinidae

There are many species in this family of sharks, but in the Mediterranean and the eastern Atlantic two species are common: **Lesser Spotted Dogfish** *(Scyliorhinus canicula)*, which measures up to a maximum of 80-90 centimetres, and **Greater Spotted Dogfish** *(Scyliorhinus stellaris)*, which can be slightly longer. These dogfish live in coastal waters at depths of 20-400 metres over all types of bottom. Both species lay eggs in rectangular horny capsules with long threads at each corner.

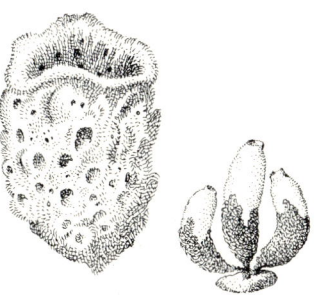

Spurdog or Picked Dogfish

These attach themselves to stones or algae.

Carcharias taurus is one of the widely distributed **Sand Sharks** and can be up to 2 metres in length. It occurs in coastal waters in West Africa, near the Canaries, the Cape Verde Islands, South Africa and in the Caribbean. It prefers a sandy bottom; with its yellowish-brown colouring it is well disguised. In summer, it will approach the shore. It is not good to eat. *Carcharias ferox*, another of the **Sand Sharks**, occurs in the eastern Atlantic, off the coast of Madeira, in the Bay of Biscay and in the Mediterranean. It can be up to 4 metres long. Its skin is reddish and it has large black spots on its back. It lives in very deep water, never resting. In summer months it will sometimes hunt among shoals of fish along the coast. It is aggressive and can be dangerous to Man.

Galeocordo cuvieri, one of the **Tiger Sharks**, is up to 6 metres in length. The young sharks of this species are tiger-like, whitish with black diagonal stripes. These markings fade later. They will eat anything and live in warm seas near the coast. They will enter the mouths of rivers and harbours in their hunt for food and, as a result, they are dangerous to bathers. Their flesh, skin and liver are of considerable economic importance.

Great White Shark
(Carcharodon carcharias)

These are aggressive sharks which can grow to a length of 12 metres and weigh up to 3 tonnes. They occur in tropical and sub-tropical, as well as temperate waters and also in the Mediterranean. They are particularly common along the southern coast of Australia, where they are a constant danger to bathers. They are regarded as the most dangerous of all the sharks. They are not eaten.

Sole *(Solea Solea)*

Soles are flatfish similar to plaice and are found over sand and mud in the Atlantic and the Mediterranean. They are 20-50 centimetres long and have flat bodies, which are pigmented only on the upper side, where both eyes are situated. Young soles are long and more fish-shaped; it is only during the various stages of their development, that the final characteristic shape of the adult fish is reached. They always swim with the pigmented side uppermost. They are extremely good to eat.

Sponges *(Porifera)*

This phylum is the simplest group of multicelled animals. Sponges are many-celled animals but their body is not made up of differentiated cell material and is sack-like in form. The walls of these "sacks" are penetrated by several closable pores, through which water is drawn into the body of the sponge. The water then flows out through an upper opening, known as the osculum. The body-mass of the sponge is supported by a skeleton of minute spicules, consisting of calcium carbonate, silica, or spongin – an elastic, horny protein related chemically to silk. Some sponges live singly, while others form large colonies. Some sponges are minute, measuring only a few millimetres, while other can measure 50 centimetres. There are also hard and soft sponges; bath sponges belong to the latter group. Nearly all sponges live in the sea. Only one family, with very few species, occurs in fresh water.

Starfish *(Asteroidea)*

This class of echinoderms are star-shaped. They have five or more arms radiating from a central point. The mouth opening is on the lower side. Their calcareous external skeleton often has spines or stumps. They move by means of sucker-like "tube-feet",

Sponges

Starfish

of which they have two rows on each arm. These tube-feet are operated by means of a complicated water vascular system. Starfish are predatory, feeding on crustaceans, molluscs and other echinoderms as well as on fish. They can cause great damage in oyster- and mussel-beds.

Sticklebacks (Gasterosteidae)
The main representative of this family is the **Three-spined Stickleback** (Gasterosteus aculeatus). This species lives in fresh water throughout Europe, Asia, North Africa and North America. It is 8 centimetres long and has three stout spines on its back. Sticklebacks prefer shallow water where there is plenty of vegetation. They are greedy predators, feeding mainly on fish spawn and young fish. During the breeding-season the males change colour, assuming a brilliantly coloured red and blue "wedding dress". The males construct round nests out of plant detritus in hollows, where they care for the young, having driven the females away.

Stone Bass (Polyprion americanum)
These fish live in the Mediterranean and the Atlantic and are 150 centimetres long and weigh 50 kilograms. They are usually found around caves and rocks and they frequent driftwood.

Sturgeon (Acipenser sturio)
These fish are related to the sharks and, since ancient times, have been regarded as a great delicacy. They occur along the Baltic coasts, in the Mediterranean and along the coasts of North America. In Spring they swim up the larger rivers to breed. They are 2-3 metres long. Sturgeon eggs preserved in salt are known as caviar and are an expensive delicacy.

Sun-fish (Mola mola)
These fish occur in tropical and subtropical water, but they have been found as migrants off the coast of Norway. They can be up to 3 metres long and weigh 3 tonnes. Their body is short and almost spherical in outline with small eyes. The bones of the jaw are formed into a sort of rostrum. Their soft flesh is not good to eat.

Sword-fish (Xiphias gladius)
The sword-fish is the only representative of its family. Its most prominent feature is the long, pointed "sword" of its elongated upper jaw. The "sword" can measure as much as a third of the total length of the fish, which may be as long as 4 metres., It has a thin body and smooth skin. It is dark blue in colour with a reddish sheen. It is found in warm and temperate waters in all seas. It is one of the fastest swimmers and the greediest predator of all the bony fish. It lives well out to sea, only approaching the coasts at breeding-time. It is then widely fished; its flesh is similar to that of tunny.

Tailed Amphibians (Caudata or Urodela)
Tailed amphibians were widely distributed in northern regions in ancient times and they still live there in large numbers. They are always elongated or cylindrical and mostly plump. In contrast with the frogs and toads (Anura), they do not lose their tail after metamorphosis. They have a bare, slimy skin, which can be either smooth, granular or warty. Many species, both aquatic and air-breathing, also respire through the skin. There are about 150 species, among the most common are the **Fire Salamander** and the **Newts**.

Tellins (Tellinidae)
The shells of these molluscs, which are very common in the Mediterranean, are only 2 centimetres long and relatively flat, and mostly broad rather than long. They are pink in colour with concentrically arranged bands. They live in sand and are eaten in large numbers in Mediterranean countries. They are related to the Veneridae or **Venus Molluscs**.

Tench (Tinca tinca)
This member of the carp family is found throughout Europe and western Asia, mainly in muddy, still, fresh water, where there is an abundance of vegetation. Tench are on average 30-40 centimetres in length and weigh between 1-3 kilograms. They have powerful bodies and bottle-green slimy skin. They are often kept in ponds, as they grow so rapidly. They are good to eat. They feed on worms, snails, lice and leeches.

Three-bearded Rockling (Onos tricirratus)
The name of this member of the cod family is derived from its three barbels or tentacles, two on the tip of the snout and one on the point of the chin. These fish are about 30 centimetres long and occur with their related species in the north-eastern Atlantic, in the Mediterranean and in the Black Sea. Like all cod, they are good to eat.

Tree-frog (Hyla arborea)
The tree-frog belongs to the Anura and occurs throughout the world. It is between 4-5 centimetres long and has a shiny green skin. It lives in bushes near water, where the female lays her eggs in great clumps, which adhere together.

Triggers (Balistidae)
A characteristic of these fish, which live among the coral reefs of the Indian ocean, is the particular shape of their dorsal fin. It consists of just three spiny rays, the first one of which is longer than the others and can be raised and locked in an upright position by means of a special trigger mechanism. When in danger, these fish will hide among the coral and lock themselves in by means of their spiny rays. They are then safely wedged and cannot be drawn out of their hiding-place. Their body is high and laterally compressed and they are 50-60 centimetres in length. Their scales are brownish-violet in colour.

Trout
Sea Trout (Salmo trutta)
This member of the salmon or trout family is 20-50 centimetres long and its greyish-blue scales have reddish or black spots. **River Trout** live in the inland waters in central and northern Europe. During the breeding-season, all trout swim up the rivers to clear mountain streams, rich in oxygen, where they lay their eggs. After breeding, they return to their original waters.
Rainbow Trout (Salmo gairdneri)
This trout is a related species and has a broad reddish stripe along its sides. It is introduced into Europe from North America at the end of the last century and is now extensively farmed. The flesh of all trout is delicately flavoured and tender.

Trunkfish (Ostracionodae)
These fish have a wedge-shaped body surrounded by a tough shell, which consists of hexagonal bony plates fused together. The tail-fins and the skin round the mouth and the anus are soft. Trunkfish have strong teeth, with which they devour the minute crustaceans and worms which they find among the coral. They only occur in tropical waters. They can move only very slowly. Although they are protected by their shell, some species defend themselves by emitting a lethal poisonous fluid. Because of their strange appearance,

Three-bearded Rockling

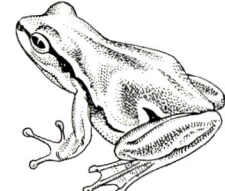

Tree-frog

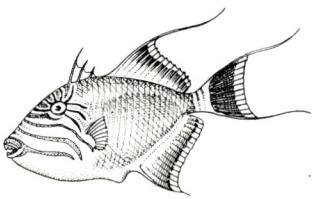

Trigger

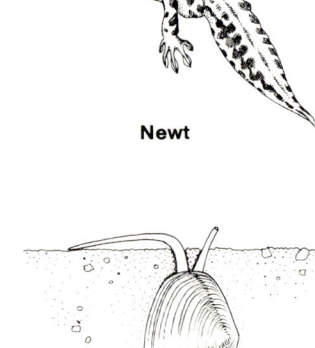

Stone Bass

Sturgeon

Newt

Tellin

they are often preserved and sold as curiosities.

Turbot *(Scophthalmus maximus)*

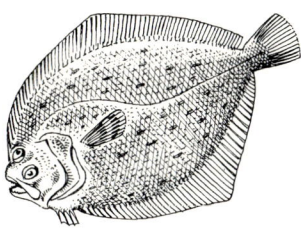

Turbot

These are flatfish with an asymmetrical, oval body with both eyes on the left. They bury themselves in the sand or gravel in fairly shallow water and their colouring acts as an excellent camouflage. They prey on crustaceans, molluscs and fish. They are very good to eat. They can be up to 90 centimetres in length and occur along the European coasts of the Atlantic and in the Mediterranean. A related species, **Brill** *(Scophthalmus laevis)* is found in the same regions, but is usually only 40 centimetres in length

Whiting *(Gadus merlangus)*

These fish are members of the cod family and occur throughout the eastern Atlantic and occasionally in the Mediterranean and the Black Sea. They are up to 60 centimetres in length. In summer, they follow the herring shoals from the north into the Channel and along the Brittany coast. They are greedy predators, feeding mainly off fish, shrimps and crabs. They are good to eat.

Whiting

Yellow-tail *(Seriola dumerili)*

These fish are members of the family of spiny mackerel *(Carangidae)* and are very good to eat. They swim very fast and are greedy predators. They occur in the Atlantic and are up to 1.6 metres in length. Their tail-fin is deeply forked and crescent-shaped. They live in deep water, but in the Spring they move to shallower water along the coast to breed.

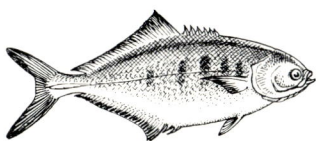

Yellow-tail

Index

(Page numbers printed in italics refer to captions and illustrations)
See also page 74 for alphabetical illustrated list of species.

Abyssal Angler Fish **40**
Acanthometron *23*
Africa
  Cane Rat in *70*
  Common Kingfisher in *61*
  European Tree Frog in *72*
  Goliath Heron in *66*
  Lakes in **12, 56**
  Lung fish in **65**
  Saddle-bill Stork *71*
  turtles on the coast of **53**
Albatross *25*
Aleutian trench *15*
alligators *61*
Alpine Newts **73**
Alvin (bathymobile) *18*
Amazon Dolphin **60**
Amazon, River **12, 62,** *62*
amphibians *66, 69,* **73**
Amphibious Sea-snake *53*
anaconda **6**
anchovies *32, 35*
Angel Fish *38,* **62,** *62,* **64**
Angler Fish **25,** *36, 40,* **40-1**
annelid worm *31*
Antarctic Ocean **12, 15, 55**
Anthozoans *33*
Anura **73**
Apoda **73**
Aral Sea **12**
Arapaima **62,** *64*
Architeuthis **41**
Arctic Ocean **12**
Arrua Turtles **61-2**
Arrow Worms **35**
Ascidiacea *32*
Asia **12,** *53, 61, 70, 72*
Astropecten *31*
Atlantic Ocean
  Amazon River and *62*
  eels crossing **54-5,** *54*
  marine basin of **12**
  ridge in **15**
  Spiny Lobster in *32*
  sturgeon in *61*
  swordfish in *21*
  turtles in **53**
  weever Fish in **50**
Atlantic tench *15*
Australia *53,* **59, 65**

back-swimmers **64,** *68*
Baltic Sea **12**
barbel *64, 65*
"Barber" Fish **49**
Bar-headed Goose *59*
barnacles *25,* **28,** *35*
barracuda *37*
Basking Shark *38*
beavers *59,* **70**
Beebe-Barton (bathysphere) *18*
Ben Franklin (submarine) *18*
benthic fish *31, 32*
Bering Sea **55**

birds
  food of **24,68,** *71*
  lakeside **59,** *59*
  pondside **70**
  prey, as *58,* **61,** *66, 70-71*
  swamps, of *71*
Black Dragonfish *41*
Black Sea *61*
bloodworms **68**
Blue and White Nile **12**
Blue Shark **39,** *39*
boa constrictor *61*
bony fish **36, 65**
boxfish *27*
Brazil **53,** *62*
British Isles *32*
Brittle Star *41*
brittleworms *29*
Butterfly Fish *44*

caddisflies **68**
California **55**
Californian Grey Whale **55**
Canary Islands *72*
Cane Rat **70**
capybara **60,** *62*
carnivores **65**
Caroline archipelago *43*
carp *58*
cartilaginous fish **26,** *27,* **38-9, 65**
Caspian Sea **12,** *61*
catfish *64*
caymans **61-2**
Central America **54**
Cerianthus membranaceus *33*
Chimera **38**
Chondrichthyes **38-9**
Clown Fish *49*
cobra *53*
cod *37*
coelenterate *43, 59*
Colombia *62*
Common Cuttlefish *31*
Common European Toad *72*
Common Kingfisher *61*
Common Necklace Shell *31*
Common Rorqual **55**
copepods *23, 23, 35*
coral *37, 42,* **43-4,** *43*
Corixa 68
Corixids **68**
cormorant *29*
Corvus marinus *29*
Cousteau, Jacques *18*
cowfish *44*
coypu **60**
crabs *25*
  food of **24**
  Hermit *37*
  inter-tidal zone, in **28,** *28*
  invertebrates, as **37,** *64*
  self-defence of **47**
cranes
crayfish **21,** *31,* **60**

crocodiles **61**
Crown of Thorns *42*
Crustacea **23, 55**
crustaceans
  food of *32*
  fresh water, in **64**
  homes of **29, 35**
  inter-tidal zones, in **28**
  lakes, in **59**
  plankton, as *23*
  ponds, in **68**
  prey, as **21,** *29,* **49, 66**
  sea-bed, on *32*
  segmented **37**
  size of **37**
cuttlefish **35, 37, 55**
Cyclops **68**

Damselfly *69*
Daphnia **68**
Dead Sea **12**
"decomposers" **24**
Deep Quest (submarine) *18*
Deep-sea Angler Fish **40**
Deepstar (bathymobile) *18*
Devil Fish *25*
Dermochelys coriacea **53**
Diving Beetle **65**
diving birds **70**
diving ducks *59*
dolphins *24, 25,* **60**
Dragon Fish **50,** *51*
dragonflies *59, 64, 65,* **68**
Duck-billed Platypus *59*
ducks *59,* **70**

earthworms **73**
East Pacific ridge *15*
Ecuador *62*
edible mussel *24*
eels **26,** *27,* **54-5,** *54,* **65**
egrets *71*
Electric Eel **62, 64**
elvers *54,* **55**
Europe
  Alpine Newts in *73*
  Common Kingfisher in *61*
  eels in **54-5**
  grass-snakes in *73*
  mackerel on **55**
  perch in *58*
  toads in *72*
  tunny-fishing in *20*
  turtles in **53**
  Viperine Snake *73*
  Water Shrew in **70**
European Tree Frog *72*

Feather Star *41*
Fighting Fish **64**
FNRS 111 (bathyscope) *18*
Fiji archipelago **43**
flamingoes *59*
flatfish **26**

flatworms **59**
flies **68**
flying-fish *25*, **35-6**, *37*
France *72*
"freshwater sharks" *69*
Frigate Bird *25*
frogs
  food of **68**
  ponds, in **66, 68**, *73*
  prey, as *59, 71, 73*
Frog Fish *47*

Ganges River Dolphin **60**
gannet *24*
gastropods **35**, *48*
geese *59*
Giant Crab **37**
Giant Shark *39*
gilt-head *25*
Glass Eel *54*
Goliath Heron *66*
grass-snakes *73*
Great Water Beetle **64**, *69*
Great White Shark **39**
grebes **59, 70**
Green Turtle *52, 53*
grouper *47*
Grunt Fish *26*
Gulf Stream **17, 55**
gulls *29, 52*
Gulper Fish *41*
guppy *60*
Guyana *62*

hake *36*
Halocentrids **40**
Halocynthia *32*
Hammerhead Shark *38*
Harvest Mouse *70*
Hawaiian ridge *15*
Hemiptera **64**, *69*
herbivores **24, 65**
Hermit Crab *37, 48*
herons *59*, **70**, *71*
herrings *5*
hippopotamus **60-1**
Horny Coral Sea Fan *43*
horse-leech *65*
Humpback Whale **55**
hydra **59**
Hyla arborea 72

Iberian peninsula *72*
iguana *52, 52*
India *53, 60,* **61**, *66*
Indian Antarctic ridge *15*
Indian Ocean **12, 43, 53**
insects
  fresh water, in **64-6**
  prey, as *29, 66, 69-72*
invertebrates
  abyssal **41**
  brightly coloured *30*
  hunters, as **35**
  inter-tidal zone, in **37**
  lakes, in **57, 64**
  migration by **55**
  predators, as **35**
  transparent **35**
Italy *72*

jabiru *71*
Japan *37*
jawless fish **65**
jelly-fish *51*
John Dory *36*

Kariba dam **56**
Kermadec trench *15*
kingfishers **59**, *61*
kittiwakes *29*
krill *37*

Labrador **15**
Labrador current **17**
Labridae *44,* **49**
Laccadive archipelago **43**
Lactoria cornuta 44
Lake Baikal **56**
Lake Malawi **56**
Lake Superior **12**
Lake Tanganyika **56**
Lake Victoria **12, 56**
lampreys *27,* **65**
Lantern Fish *41*
Leathery Turtle **53**
leeches **59**
Left-eyed Flatfish *47*
Leptocephali **55**
Lesser Spotted Dogfish *38,* **39**
limpets **28**, *28*
lizard *52*
lobster *24, 37*
Loch Ness **56**
Lung Fish **65**

mackerel **21, 55**
Maldive archipelago **43**
mammals
  aquatic species of **60**
  cuttlefish hunted by *31*
  dependence on water of **60, 70**
  difficulty of tracking **55**
  food of **68**
  prey, as *58,* **61, 71**
  remains of *62*
mantas **38-9**
Marianas trench **15**, *15*
Marsh Terns **70**
may-fly **65**
Mediterranean Sea *20-1, 32, 33,* **50, 53, 61**
Mexico **55**
mid-Atlantic ridge **15**, *15*
mid-Indian ridge *15*
mid-Pacific ridge *15*
Mirror Carp **65**
Mississippi-Missouri, River **12, 61**
mites **64**
Mollusca **55**
molluscs
  barnacles and *28*
  inter-tidal zone, in *28*
  invertebrates, as **37**
  lakes, in **64**
  limpets *28*
  Natica alderi 31
  plankton, as *23*
  prey, as *60*
monkfish *38*
Moray Eel **49**, *51*
mosquito **64**, *65*
moths **65**
mussels *21, 24,* **28, 31, 37**

Natica alderi 31
Natrix maura 73
Neon Tetras **62**, *62, 64*
Nepa **69**
New Guinea *61*
newts **59, 68, 73**
Nile, River **12**
Noctiluca 23
North America **12, 53**
Notonecta *68*

oar-fish *41*
Ob-Irtysh, River **12**
octopus **37**, *46*
omnivores **65**
otters **59-60**
owls *70*
oysters **37**

Pacific-Antarctic ridge **15**
Pacific Ocean
  archipelagos in **43**
  Common Kingfisher in *61*
  marine basin of **12**
  seals in **55**
  trench in **15**
  turtles in **53**
Pacific Salmon **55**
Painted Turtles **61**
Papuan islands *60*
Parocentrotus lividus 32
parasites **49, 65**
Peacock Worm *31*
Pearly Nautilus *37*
Pelagic Squid *41*
pelicans *59*
Peru *62*
Peru-Chile trench *15*
Philippines Islands **36**
Philippines trench **15**, *15*
pike *58,* **65**
Pilot Fish *39,* **49**
piranhas **62**, *62,* **65**
pipefish *31*
plaice *31,* **36**
planarians **59**
polychaetes **29**
polyps *42, 43*
Pond Skaters **64**, *65*
pond snail **65**
porbeagle *39*
Porcupine Fish *47*
Portuguese Man o' War **51**
prawns *41*
predators
  anchovies and *32*
  aphotic zone, in **15**
  beetles as *69*
  biological balance kept by *58*
  Common Cuttlefish as *31*
  deception of **46-7**
  reptile **61**, *73*
  salps and **35**
  toads and *72*
  warnings to **26, 50**
Pseudemys scripta 73
Puerto Rican trench **15**, *15*
puffer-fish *27*

Rabbit Fish **38**
radiolarians *23*
Rainbow Fish *44*
Ramshaw Snail *68*
rays **38, 65**
Red Mullet *36*
Red Sea **12**
Red-eared Turtle *73*
Red Scorpion Fish *47*
Red Sturgeon **36**
Remora **49**
reptiles **52-3**, *73*
River Crayfish **60**
rodents **60**, *65*
rudd *65*
ruffe *64*
Russia **12**

Saddle-bill Stork *71*
Saqitta setosa 35
salmon *21, 27,* **55**, *55,* **65**
salps **23, 35**
sandpipers **70**
Sandshark *39*
sardines *21,* **35**
Sargasso Sea **54, 65**
Scaly Dragonfish *41*
scavengers *26*
Scorpion Fish *51*
Sea Anemones *25, 33,* **37**, *37,* **43**, *43, 48,* **49, 59**
Sea Bream *25*

"Sea Crow" *29*
Sea Cucumber *37, 49*
seagulls *25*
sea-lions **55**
sea-pen *40*
sea-perch **47**
sea-snakes *53*
Sea Squirts *32*
Sea Urchins **23**, *25*, **28**, **32**, **47**
seahorse *31*
seals **55**
Selachii *38*
Sepia *31*
sharks **24**, *25*, *32*, *38*, **38-9**, **49**, **65**
shell-fish *21*
shrimps **50**, **68**
Silver Bell *41*
snails *59*, **68**
snakes **52-3**, **61**
Snipe Fish **47**
sole **26**, *27*, **47**
Solenichthyes *31*
South America **53**, **60-2**, **65**
Spain **21**
Sperm Whales **41**
Spiders *72*
Spiky Rat **70**
Spiny Eel *40*
Spiny Lobster *32*, **37**
Spiny Ray **39**
Sponges *33, 40*
squid *25*, **41**, *41*

Squirrel Fish **40**
Sri Lanka *53, 60*
Star *18*
starfish *31-2, 42*
Stargazer *40,47*
sting-ray **50**
Stomia **41**
Stone Fish *51*
Straits of Messina *21*
sturgeon *61*
Sucker Fish **49**
Sumatran Barbel *64*
sunfish **26**, *27*
Surgeon Fish **50**
swans *59*
swordfish *21*, *25*, **36**, *37*, *64*

tadpoles *60, 68, 73*
tench *65*
terrapin *73*
Thornback Ray **39**
Three-spined Stickleback *65*
thresher *39*
Tiger Sharks *38*, **39**
toads *72*
Tongan trench *15*
tope *38*
Trieste (bathyscope) **18**, *18*
Trigger Fish **50**
Tripod Fish *40*
trout *59*, *65*
Trumpet Fish **47**

trunkfish *44*
tunny *20*, *25*, **35**, *36*
turtles *25*, **52-3**, **55**, **61**

United States of America *73*
Urochordata **23**
Urodela **73**

Venezuela *62*
vertebrates **26**, **36**, **64**
Viper-fish *40*
Viperine Snake *73*
Virgin Islands *18*
voles *58*

waders *59*, **70**
water-beetles **68**
water-boatmen *59*, **64**, *65*, *68*
Water Scorpion *65*, *69*
watershrews **60**, *70*
water-snakes *72*
water voles **60**
Weever Fish **50**
Whalebone Whale **24**
whales *25*, **35**, **55**
White Shark *39*
worms **29**, **49**, **68**, *70*, *72*
wrasse *44*, **49**

Zebra Fish *64*
zooplankton **23-4**, *23*, **27**